Contents

Introduction ... ix

Part One

1. Distractions ... 3
2. Childhood ... 9
3. Searching Within ... 11
4. Speaking as a Man ... 13
5. Mom Said to Play ... 15
6. Life is a Game ... 19
7. Basic Training ... 21
8. Life Lessons ... 23
9. Life as a Martial Art ... 27
10. After the Army ... 29
11. Speaking to Myself ... 33
12. Cooling the Fiery Mind ... 37
13. Stored Memories ... 39
14. Deep Tissue Work ... 43
15. Spiritual Practice ... 47
16. Vision Quest ... 51
17. Medicine Wheel ... 63
18. The Inner Child ... 73
19. Time ... 77
20. Saturday ... 79
21. Life Purpose ... 83
22. Super Rich ... 87

Part Two

23. Lessons from Life's Journey ... 91
24. Cycles ... 95
25. Balance Through Alignment ... 99
26. Free Will ... 105
27. Dreams That Bring Goodness to All ... 109
28. Beliefs & Awareness ... 113
29. Finding Our Center ... 115
30. Mother and Me ... 119
31. The Other Side ... 125
32. Masks ... 129
33. The River ... 133
34. Floating Downstream ... 137
35. Conversation ... 141
36. Reincarnation ... 143
37. Our Choice ... 147
38. The Passing ... 149

Part Three

39. Sunday Papers ... 161

Chapter 1 ... 209

Acknowledgments ... 211
About the Author ... 213
Also by Michael Carroll ... 215

Introduction

I was discharged from the Army In January of 1973 after convincing the military command that I was unfit to continue training to kill other human beings. My beliefs at the time about God, heaven and hell were limited to the teachings of the Catholic Church during the 50's and 60's. All I knew at the time was that there was more to life than what I had been taught growing up. The books *Jonathan Livingston Seagull*, *The Teachings of Don Juan*, and *Be Here Now*, along with the music by the Moody Blues were my first teachers.

One night I was working the door at a small weekend music venue in Gainesville, Florida. That evening a band from Taos, New Mexico, the Heart Glow Trio, played. They spoke of their Teacher / Guru. Two years later I found my way to Taos and became a disciple of the Guru Herman Rednick, who taught The Christ Path of Love and Service.

There were a few rules and requirements: no meat,

no drugs, no alcohol. Every Sunday we were given a lesson to ponder, and meditate upon. We were asked to write a short paper that we would read out loud in class on the following Sunday. Those short writing assignments appear in *Part Three - Sunday Papers*. This experience was a pivotal part of my spiritual journey. Herman passed in 1985.

Several years later I attended a shaman medicine ways workshop. The teachings and ways of the Medicine Wheel, vision quests, and journeying into the world of power animals spoke clearly to me. This was like the path of love and service, but in a totally different format. This became the next stage of my journey.

Seasons change and after 10 years with Herman and 15 years with the medicine ways my inner voice said, "it's time to integrate the two paths into one." This book is my story.

Part One

Ask, and it will be given to you; seek, and you will find; knock and the door will be opened to you.

Jesus, Matthew 7:7

Distractions

We live in a world of distractions. The invention of the "news" has grown from word of mouth to newspapers, and now we have instant Internet communication with the World Wide Web.

If we look at the general health of humanity and planet Earth, we might ask, "When will we start to heal?" One answer is, "When we set in motion a plan to end wars on all levels." Once that's in motion, everything will start to improve. Of course, everything starts within the individual, and when enough individuals hold a vision, that vision starts to manifest. This is easy to see on both the black and white sides of manifestation. Selfishness can be evil if we use our desire and power over others in a negative way. Look what white Americans did to the Native Americans and to African Americans.

It's all part of our humanity. The "us against

them" mentality is nothing new. It's simply re-manifesting in relationship to the population and consciousness on earth. Remember 2000 years ago the population of the world was around 300 million, or roughly the population of the United States in 2000. Worldwide we are now close to 8 billion. The population of the world's developed countries is currently a little over 1.3 billion people, which is about 17% of the world population today and will be about 50% of the world population by 2050.

According to WorldVision.org, 24% of the world's population, which equates to 1.9 billion people, live in impoverished conditions and dire circumstances. By 2030, more than half of the world's poor will live in what they term fragile contexts. https://www.google.com/url?sa=t&source=web&rct=j&opi=89978449&url=https://www.worldvision.org/sponsorship-news-stories/global-poverty-

How long do we think this will take to turn around and start healing? If we bring astrology into the mix, we recently ended the Piscean age that began around the biblical time of Christ. Some estimate that we have entered the age of Aquarius in the last 50-100 years. Aquarius is also referred to as "the age of light." Each of the twelve astrological ages lasts approximately 2160 years as part of the Grand Year of the precession of the equinoxes.

According to some ancient Mayan esoteric beliefs, Alcyone is the central star of the Pleiadean star system, and our sun is the outermost star of this system. The

Mayan Great Cycle is a calendar that delineates the 26,000 year-long cycle of our Sun and Solar System around Alcyone. Some people speculate that our Sun is moving into something called a "photon belt," or belt of light particles. As we move deeper into this photon belt, we are moving into the Age of Light described in many ancient prophecies, including the Maya.

According to this view, we began to penetrate the Photon Belt in 1972, though we were only touching the edges. What does the age of light mean? With light the illusion of darkness is dispelled. Within the light we discover that we are eternal. In the light we realize that time as we know it on the physical plane doesn't exist. Within the light we no longer have dark nights. Instead, everything is simply glowing of its own light without wires and a generating station. Nothing needs to sleep because the body is made of eternal light vibration.

Eventually, humanity must heal. We have had great teachers along the way. The Christ is the latest world teacher for humanity. He planted the seed and added the quality of love to the Buddha's earlier teaching of wisdom. Christ is the embodiment of Love and Wisdom. The Christ was the world teacher/avatar for the age of Pisces, the Fishes, and Jesus represented the office of the Christ in the spiritual Hierarchy. According to the Tibetan master Djwal Khul, it will be the Lord Maitreya, who will be the avatar for the new age of Aquarius.

We are responsible for the state of the world. We are the ones who must change. Leaders come and go for both the light and dark side. The dark side relishes power over people, while the light side seeks to bring balance to humanity.

Humans are here to become conscious that they are a soul. We have been created by God consciousness in some realm we are yet fully aware of. However, one thing is for sure, everything seems to have speeded up. Now we can send messages and images around the world is a few seconds. Imagine what things were like 500, a 1000, even 2000 years back to the time when Christ walked the earth.

In the energy of the world that we live in, the body needs to sleep. When we sleep, our consciousness often leaves the physical body. We literally leave the physical though we remain connected by what is called the silver cord. The cord allows us to return to our physical body when we wake up. When the physical, passes, the cord is separated in a flash or a slow fade away.

Ok, then what? Well, it depends where we are within our consciousness. Imagine if our body didn't need anything to keep it running? No need for rest, food, or sleep. If that was the case, there would be no such thing as tomorrow or next year. It just is until we decide to change whatever "It" is. We try to put into words that the eternal exists now.

We don't have a soul; we are a soul. And the soul has a body. We are a soul having a physical or "lower" experience. By lower we refer to the physical, mental, and emotional aspects of the human soul experience.

Once we figure something out, we no longer need to give it the same amount of attention, we simply see, feel, and understand. We paid extra attention when we learned to drive a car, but over time it became automatic. We can talk or listen to music and still pay full attention to the road. We are multi-dimensional beings, and our brain is like a receiver that pulls in waves of energy from our inner dimensions. This is like a computer connecting to the internet. We choose what we want to pay attention to. This is our free will.

Imagine if when the Sun sets it doesn't get dark, instead, everything glows of its own light from within. Our physical eye somehow expanded its limited visual light spectrum. If you ever looked through an infrared or night vision glasses, you get the idea. This is the reason so much focus is on "the light." Christ is the light and the Way.

This is a glimpse into the inner world. Who we are when we take away the physical body is the state of our consciousness. If we knew the reality of when we die, we might discover that from the bigger perspective, we would be happy for the relief death brings and dread being born again. It's almost funny to look at from that perspective. A soul being born into a baby's body is no easy task. How many years does it take before you can take care of yourself? At death we are set free from the confines of this physical plane world.

Childhood

Growning up, it was rare to get scolded or spanked. I can remember two pants down spankings. One by the hand and the other with a belt. I can't remember exactly what I did to deserve it, but I do remember that whatever I did, it was over the line. I knew it, and I deserved the punishment and scolding. A little like getting an electric shock from the 110 outlets, it's a very quick pain and then gone, lesson learned. I never held it against my Mom. Dad never touched me or my brothers in that way.

Strong uncomfortable emotions were somehow always kept at low tide, unless they were happy emotions. There were many gatherings for cocktails and dinner with *Crème de Menthe* or *Creme de Cacao* with desert. I was always allowed to have a little sip of my favorite, *Crème de Menthe*.

On Saturday night I was often left alone to watch

TV shows of my choice and eat ice cream and or cookies. We never had soda in the house, it was well water, orange, or grape juice, and sometimes lemonade. My parents never pushed anything on me that I can recall. They can tell you what and how you are supposed to be in this life. I didn't get that feedback.

There was so much alcohol in the house that it was easy during my high school years to take a little out of each bottle and pour it into a small empty peanut butter jar. I learned to guzzle it down and get a buzz. It only took a few times puking, and one time passing out, to learn my lesson.

Searching Within

Reading and spelling were never a strong point in my school experience. I graduated every year by the "skin of my teeth" as I was often told by teachers. In 1963, on the last day of fifth grade in Catholic school, I read the words "repeat 5th grade." Everyone on the bus ride home asked me "did you get promoted or left back?"

I responded to everyone "I am too afraid to look" and put up some form of energetic shield as only an eleven-year-old can do. When I walked into the house mom told me that she talked to the local Memorial School Principal and I would go into sixth grade in September. My integrity was saved!

I finished high school with a 1.6 average and got accepted into Paterson state college because I was a good high school track pole-vaulter. My parents did not and would not pay the $225 dollar fall semester tuition because they believed I would flunk out. That summer between high school and college I worked as a lifeguard at the local pool and made enough to pay the tuition. My parents were right.

Two years almost to the day from high school graduation I was drafted into the army. A week later President Nixon signed the bill that draftees would no longer go to Vietnam. The idea of going to Vietnam never entered my mind and going through basic training was viewed like an athletic training and a flash back to playing army with air rifles and cap guns. as kids.

My focus growing up was playing and consciously adapting to the change of seasons. Ice skating, sled riding, to spring baseball, swimming and fishing, building tree forts, playing war as we watched on TV, and then girls were added.

After basic training I was confronted with an abrupt life river current shift and woke up to the reality that I was getting trained to kill other humans. I realized this was simply unacceptable. This was the beginning of searching within for answers and clarity to understand life's meaning.

Speaking as a Man

July 23, 2010

Because our culture does not encourage sensitivity in a man does not mean it is not there. A man has incredible ability to stay in the mind without going into his feeling nature. Most men are unwilling to express or feel emotion in a sensitive way because they are disconnected from the female part of their nature.

When tears flow, it is not the thoughts that I hear but the feelings that I feel that change the course of my direction to see clearly what's in the mind's eye. We also need to be able to feel the winds in the air and the currents in the water when the tears flow. Feelings can override thoughts in the same way that thoughts can override feelings. There is a place of balance where feelings and thoughts intersect.

Just because you are a guy doesn't mean you don't

have the nature of a woman. Simply because the culture does not develop the sensitivity in a man does not mean it is not there. It would be better to seek answers than to get blindsided and knocked out. A man can burn and in his fire while a woman can float in her water and swim within herself.

A man can deny his feelings with the overriding mental facility. He can go into, "I don't feel anything mode," which is impossible as long as you have a heart. Something blocks his ability to feel. A fiery mind is hard to cool and only in the cooling can a man enter the water like a red hot iron that cools in the bubbles. Because the water cannot touch the fire when it is too hot it needs to be cooled. The slow deep waters are places where we have no choice but to look, see, and hear what is going on in inside.

Mom Said to Play

When we were young, we often spread our arms so we could ride the wind in our imagination and jump in puddles and feel the water. We delighted in the feelings of our play as we explored ourselves and the physical world around us.

Then, in a few short years, we started to feel the pulse of our culture and hear the morning bell directing us to our desk. Some go willingly, others kicking and screaming, but we all climb on the conveyor belt to be integrated into the social system. This system creates the present state of our general populace. The foundation of which is a mix of governing laws and money. How we live and move in this system can be the difference between living a life of love or a hell.

Clearly the populace is waking up to the rumbles and shakes within the fabric that holds us. No longer can we ride on the wind and laugh at getting wet in the rain. The joy started to slip away when our attention was directed to the accumulation of material wealth for our supposed happiness.

The simple basics we were taught at a young age of sharing and playing nice are not expected when we step off the conveyor belt into the workaday world. The laws of the system do not require it, and we discover that our play time and childhood were converted into hours on the job.

Most are content to follow along with the program when material dreams are within reach and attainable. It has a different feeling when you are not happy inside the material dream. With the fabric of our world shaking, and people fighting off depression, it is easy to see how our childhood foundation was undermined and replaced with misleading information. Instead of honoring and protecting our childlike nature as we get older, instead we disregard it. Like cutting the roots of a tree and hoping it will still produce fruit.

The role of our child changes as we transition into adulthood, but it does not disappear. Like parents protecting their children from the harsh realities of adult life, we need to protect and continue nurturing our child self as we age. This transition process is serious business because a happy child within is required to be a healthy adult facing the outside world.

When I was young and struggling in school, the common wisdom of the day was to keep the kid in after school and make him study. My mother told the teacher "I will not take away Michael's playtime." That still rings in my ear. No one understood Dyslexia at the time, but Mom's intuition provided the support necessary to prevent me from falling into the pits of humiliation. Playtime at any age is like rain to the garden that nourishes our roots and refreshes our attitude as we face difficult times.

In all of life, depression is the hardest to deal with. We spend billions on antidepressant drugs and seek external desires when the simple fact is the opposite of depression. It's not work or lack of money, it is play and joy.

The ability to play as a child is a gift of grace. In an adult, it is a developed skill that is so pleasurable and beneficial that it sits right next to the art of love and creativity. When we recognize this truth, we are left with no choice but to reevaluate our purpose. Believing that we are here to enjoy ourselves or to remember how to do so is not a far-fetched idea. It is an essential component of a whole person.

Life is a Game

Life is referred to as a game because there are rules and consequences for our actions on all three levels of our being. Karma, or reaping what we sow, is one of the most basic universal laws-- the law of cause and effect. What we often don't talk about is how that same law applies in the mental and emotional vibrational reality. How does the reaping and sowing affect us on emotional and mental planes?

If we treat someone badly and hurt them mentally or emotionally, it is not usually detected by human laws. Why? Because we presently lack the ability to see fully into the mental and emotional worlds and pull out the memory card, replaying exactly what had taken place. We might believe we are getting away with whatever we are doing, but it's all recorded.

That's not hard to imagine if we remember what humans have developed in the computer world over the last fifty years—it's all eternal. Our physical body is not much different than our pet dog or cat. Everything has a certain life span. Even rocks wear down, oceans move around as Earth shifts over billions of years.

Basic Training

Summer of 1972

The Vietnam War was the current conflict when I was drafted in the summer of 1972. War was the seamless next step after playing army with toy guns as a child. Shooting real guns for the first time and throwing hand grenades was fun because my innocent nature never registered that I might actually kill someone. I had a very competitive athletic nature and found a home in the physical training. My attention focused on getting in top shape to have a shot at the physical fitness award. Then on graduation day and full glory, I was singled out in front of 200 men with the highest score of my platoon. I received the trophy in one hand and in the other hand my orders for advanced training.

I remember reading the words "infantry training" and feeling the shock to my system. With a jolt of awareness, I realized I needed to get out. The enjoyment was gone, and within a few days I was being trained in the art of ambushing the enemy. I was lying on my stomach covered with camouflage and holding an M16 when we heard the order to fire. The training weapons, filled with blanks, cracked all around. I refused to fire and when I was told I was disobeying a direct order I rolled on my back and fired into the air.

The big drill Sergeant popped off his chest and said,"It's people like you that get others killed in war." I replied, "I don't plan to get in that situation drill Sergeant."

I didn't plan to fire into the air, but it happened spontaneously when I saw another human at the end of my rifle. It felt like I was taken over by a force within me that I had never experienced. I simply rejected the situation as if my soul intervened with my unaware personality. It was as if I had woken up in the middle of a dream with no mom, dad, or brother around to help me out.

Life Lessons
A Soldier's Hope

I often meet a person on the street who asks, "What's happening?" I reply, "Everything."

I remember being on an army post when a lonely soldier, with a ray of hope and light in his eyes, asked my friend, "What's happening?" My friend answered, "Nothing."

The light in the soldier's eyes quickly dimmed as he withdrew into himself. His face became downcast, and the hope faded.

I learned a great lesson in that moment—we can make a difference. A smile, a beam of love, consciously reaching out to others around us, especially those who have reached out to us, is what life is about. I love everyone and while a sense of dislike and fear may arise when I see someone who seems to be violent, I realize it is my personality that is judging and seeing only his personality. At the same time, my soul sees his soul, and from this place I can love. Within my soul consciousness I touch everyone I meet.

From the soul's perspective, one life is just a day in God's school, and that my friend, is another reason why judgment is such a sharp double-edged sword. If we knew all of the circumstances behind someone else's actions or situation we would not judge. We would see it for what it is.

With a calm mind and loving heart, the eternal soul consciousness has a vehicle to bring its light and presence into the outer world. This is entirely up to the individual, and much depends on what part of the world's culture we were raised in and our purpose for this life. This does not mean we are a pushover in the world. With a calm mind and loving heart, one starts to see from the soul's perspective. We become a channel for our soul's consciousness into the world. Rather, we could see and have more compassion. Always having love in one's heart with a calm mind does not mean we are a push over (so to speak) in the world.

We will find our conscious self can seek and discover the kingdom of God. What does within mean? In a nutshell, it is the eternal world that exists within our consciousness, the part of us that is not this physical body. This is the part of us that can drift off into dream land much like we do when we fall asleep.

It is not much different than driving our car to the mountains, the beach, work, or to the store. We have many options and directions to choose from. This is our free will, and how our free will actions affect others brings the law of karma into play. Or, as Christ taught, "we reap what we sow."

Choices need to be made all the time in this physical world. We choose what we do for a living, who we live with, what our responsibilities are, what we eat and drink, and generally how we interact and maintain our balance on all three levels while living in the world.

How do we navigate our journey in the river current of life? We have experienced all levels of river flow from calm, clear, and gentle to ragging rapids. We have survived to where we are in relationship to the here and now.

We have our body, our emotions, and the feelings that follow our mental thought processes. We are in the world, and we are within ourselves. We have relationships with others and with ourselves. That is one key of many along our pathway to balance through alignment. In many ways we are free to choose our path. If we want to go somewhere else, we must visualize it, we must want it, feel it, and seek it, otherwise the life current still flows.

We strive for some form of harmony, otherwise it can get very uncomfortable, which is usually a sign that we have something to bring into alignment. This could be as simple as avoiding a boulder on a road, or the log sticking out of the water, while trying to navigate through rough waters. This is why we need a foundation to build on.

Spirituality brings greater understanding,

consciousness, and love to a human life. Spirituality is our personal practice in daily life, be it meditation, work, home, or social interactions. It is intertwined with our thoughts, emotions, and deeds in the world and within our internal personal consciousness. Spirituality is constantly refining our awareness to be more understanding, loving, harmless in our thoughts, words, and deeds.

Life as a Martial Art

Martial arts students begin with a white belt and move through different colored ranks while gaining experience enough to support a black belt of the first degree. All levels of attainment require focus and discipline. It is the energetic quality of the focus and discipline that leads a person along the path of life.

We are responsible for where we are today. We are the ones who can change ourselves from within. Like maps and road signs along highways and city streets we can learn to read the inner signs that we come across in our mental nature or feelings. We can look at the inner map and imagine or dream about what we would like. Then ponder how to make those dreams manifest. Our ability to dream is taking place in a different realm than the physical body.

Our work is to do our daily practice and put it to the test. It is easy to stay calm when the atmosphere is calm. Staying calm amid humanity's turmoil, on the Internet, friends' dramas, neighbors, family, children, grandchildren, and spouses. Can we remain, or work towards, having a calm mind and loving heart? Is that not the ultimate purpose of being a human? With a calm mind and loving heart, the eternal soul consciousness has a vehicle to bring its presence into the world.

Jesus the Christ was a living example. At the core of Christ's teaching we discover the eternal love and light of reality, the place where our soul resides. Our work is to train our body mind and emotions to be a channel for our soul in the world. We begin to realize that our true self is our eternal soul and that our soul is the core behind the teaching to, "Store your treasures in heaven where the moths and thieves can't steal it." (Matthew 6: 19-21). We cannot take any physical world riches with us when the body dies. We are here to live and intermingle with our physical emotional and mental reality. How we do that will be reflected in our "life review" that takes place after death.

If we are receptive to the life review, the guides on the other side will help us plan for the next incarnation. We will reincarnate into a family situation where we have an opportunity to reach or experience the needed lessons or opportunities, we need to awaken the soul or pay back some karmic dues. It's hard sometime to not be judgmental. We reap what we sow, and as a result we create our environment, individually, as a nation, and as a world.

After the Army

On the train ride from New Jersey to Gainesville Florida in January of 1974 I read a story. Jesus was walking along the path with his disciples when they came upon a dead dog full of maggots. The disciples turned away in disgust, but Jesus looked at the dog and said, "His teeth are white as pearls. There is something good to be found in everything if you look deeply enough." I was touched by his attitude.

Feeling clueless about my life, I began to ask myself. "What am I doing here, what's the point?" I heard a voice say, "Now is the time when parents and culture said, "It was time to work 40 hours a week for the next 45 years." Another voice spoke from the inside, "No way, there has to be more to it."

I asked everyone around me, "What is going on, and why are we alive? What are we here to do?" No one had answers and most became uncomfortable with my questions. The Catholic religion did not answer my questions.

In my mind, like the snap of a finger, I saw childhood playmates disappearing from the banks of the river where we played. They took the bait and were reeled inland toward the mass consuming culture with only two weeks of vacation a year. It freaked me out to think that I could be reeled in like that.

In my vision, I turned and walked into the river, deeper and deeper until the current pulled my feet off the bottom. In the river I began to feel like a child born into a new world. Always pleasurable until the river picked up speed. With no feet on the ground my thoughts ran wild with the current.

I felt lost and reached out to the cosmos for help. Books started to appear, and I soon discovered what I was feeling was not unusual. I felt like the character Jonathan Livingston Seagull when he first left the flock in Richard Bach's book of the same name. With no attraction to religion, I read the Bible and discovered that Jesus was not talking about religion but about a way of life.

I was introduced to his simple version of karma when he said, "You reap what you sow." I felt an attraction to the concept that if we seek the Kingdom within first, all the rest shall be given. At the time, I was seeking internal answers and took what was being given as a good sign to continue letting the river take me downstream.

The concept of karma and reincarnation explained

how the reaping of our sowed actions in one life could be carried over to another life. This opened my mind to existing worlds that are not visible to the naked eye. We are within a conscious framework, and we are responsible for the beliefs we hold and the waves we create. We can fool ourselves and get into some difficult situations. We may not wish to appear out of balance or delusional, yet to those who can see nothing is hidden. Seeking that which is beyond the need to live is a fine line to walk, and what we do in our spare time alters the direction of our lives.

Speaking to Myself

April 9, 2011

Becoming alive and centered on all levels makes us multi-level conscious beings. When we talk about finding peace or holding our center, we are talking about the general working condition of our body, mind, and emotions. Being highly focused is not the same as being centered with nothing in the outer world to hold onto. I jumped directly into the unknown with the innocence and trust of a child. It was unavoidable; I dared to believe that there was more to it than they were telling me.

Everything began to make sense as I realized there were no accidents. Wishing for peace and seeking peace are not the same. As any good river runner knows, sooner or later there will be rapids and we must be prepared for the unexpected. The river guide does not cry or pout when conditions change. Instead, a wise guide puts on proper clothes and gears up to face what comes.

It is the same in life except we are not all experienced river guides. Most of us are not prepared to deal with the tightening of canyon walls or increased water speed. Life's rapids drag our feet and having mental and emotional fits because things are not unfolding the way we planned is counterproductive--it's probably no accident.

These challenges are likely part of the growth curriculum for our life. Our purpose is to learn how the universe works in the third dimension and our inner reality is the direct result of our belief structure. When we come from the perspective of our grounded clear self, we see external events unfolding like a movie, the story of our life. We have developed ways to avoid what we must eventually face. We have to let thoughts and feelings go like we let the river flow through our legs.

Have you ever had an argument with yourself that won't stop? It's one thing to have disturbing discussion with a person across the table and another to continue that conversation when you're home alone. Everyone knows the experience, it can last for hours, days, weeks and years, depending on our ability to let it go. If we learn our lessons, the next time the situation presents itself, we will step through the experience while holding mental and emotional clarity. We will move through the experience like a master of movement. How we resolve these inner battles this time determines the playing field next time we are presented with a similar situation.

There is a huge issue around trust that we must integrate into our life. Much depends on the wisdom, clarity of mind, and dreams we hold, finding the line between trust and stupidity can be a difficult lesson. As we trust that life will lead us to our true self we need to leave the trusting home of the child. We must travel a different direction, discovering who we are. Our ability to objectively witness our out-of-control mind is where we will find our center--the wise voice within.

How do we know if it is really the wise voice during those sleepless nights when the thoughts and emotions are running wild? It is never fun. Sometimes they are on the extreme edge and are so stimulating that we lose our ability to be present in our daily life.

The time comes when we wake up, realizing that we are living and standing somewhere in the middle of the eternal Universe. We may wake up and realize, "I am stuck in a belief pattern that keeps me focused on material gain." When we stopped thinking about that we distracted ourselves by focusing on something else. TV is one of our favorite distractions. It entertains our consciousness until we are tired and fall asleep. Other distractions include thinking about money and our financial situation, or maybe we fantasize about what we would like to purchase that we believe will make us happy on some level. These are necessary distractions because we do need to earn a living.

When I was 20, I started to hear a voice inside my

head and felt a great desire to understand the purpose of life. My religion had taught me that heaven was a place you go to when you die if you were lucky enough to avoid purgatory, or worse yet hell. The culture offers pills to fight depression if the burden upon oneself is an internal matter.

Cooling the
Fiery Mind

July 18, 2010

A fiery mind is hard to cool down, and only in the cooling can one enter the water. The slow, deep waters are where we have no choice but to look and hear what is going on inside. There is nothing to do but absorb the vibe. Most women can cry at the drop of the hat while men need the wave to sweep over them to recognize tender emotion. The cold man is just the man who went to the ice to get numb instead of jumping in the water with his lady--it is a huge difference. A woman is at home in the water even if the waters are turbulent. The man is completely out of his element in his emotions. In most cases, he would rather stand on the ice and not feel the emotion in the room, which gives an illusion of control.

As an adult our ability to be lighthearted and

become as children is as critical to our overall well-being as water, light, and temperature are to growing food. Without a healthy relationship with our inner kid, we cannot be a healthy person or planet. The writing was on the wall if one took time to read it. Now the oil is on the water for all to see. I ask, "Where is our child?" When the children are happy the adults are happy. There can be no compromise on this. True sadness is the suffering of the children who are out of sight and out of mind. Ignoring this is no longer an option. The present system has the average populace watching three to four hours of TV a day in mindless denial.

Stored Memories

One Saturday morning, when I was 4 or 5, I looked out the upstairs window and saw a moving van next door. When I asked about the truck in Kevin's driveway, I was told they were moving. The only person I knew my size was taken away, and I was led to believe it was not a big deal. It was an early lesson in life, "that it was okay to let things go." I was pretty much a free spirit because my brothers were years older and they already tired out my parents.

When I look back now, I wonder, "Where did I store that memory? In my shoulders? How deep did it go?" It must be someplace where there is a lot of pain because it really hurts. It is sharp and intense--I scream at the top of my lungs when the body worker hits a spot. At times it hurts my throat. Then I am reminded that I should make the sound come out of my stomach. That feels the pain somewhere deep in my body, not in my throat. Kevin, my little friend, was taken away without a feeling of compassion from my family.

What did that teach me? Somewhere on the way to that answer, I remembered what happened to me when I pulled the coffee percolator full of hot coffee over on my 16-month-old body. How was it that I pulled the cord at that age? I was curious about everything. The cord was hanging down the front of the counter, and I pulled hard.

When liquid fire touched my face, I moved to the left as the hot coffee poured over my right shoulder and down my back. Blinded with pain, screaming was all I could do. What experience could I, or did I, retreat into? What place in my mind did I find that was safe? To what place of feeling other than pain could I go?

Did I leave my body for a time? Did the angels of compassion take me away? Who was there for me? Who could touch me in my body that was wrapped from head to toe? Would I trust anyone? That seems like a raw deal. The words don't connect with the feelings. The pain from the scars is so intense on my shoulder that it takes me out of my mind and into my feelings. Pain and freedom come together in this process.

People around me felt bad that I was burned, and my mom felt guilty. But no one spoke about how they felt. What about me? How did I feel? I was taught not to make a big deal out of it. I was offered the opportunity to have my scars sanded off, but I refused because they told me it would be painful. I didn't want to go through the pain just so I wouldn't have to worry about what people might think of my scars. I could live with it. When people asked, I just told them I pulled a coffee pot on myself. I remember being self-conscious later when summertime brought girls in bathing suits into my awareness.

Deep Tissue Work

When the therapist looked me in the eye and asked, "How can you smile when someone is expressing so much pain?" I didn't have an answer. It was rare to be called out my behavior. Smiling, I now know, was how I learned to cope and insulate myself from uncomfortable feelings. The smile would pop me up and out of a turbulence like a life jacket in water, allowing me to stay in my mind. The smile was a mask and a defense.

Some time passed after that smiling session with a therapist when I was introduced to the breath work called rebirthing. The practice began with sitting on pillows, pulling in a breath like an archer pulls back the bow, and then letting the breath out fast as one lets the arrow fly. In and out the practitioner gently reminded me to continue to breathe.

Was it 5 minutes or 15? I'm not sure, but all of a sudden I was 16 months old, playing under my family's kitchen table. I was walking from one chair to another, staying out of the way while the party guests were busy clearing the dinner plates and getting ready for dessert and coffee. I noticed a rope dangling from the counter and ventured across the room to grab hold. I held on with my left hand grabbed with my right and pulled a little harder for support.

I was greeted with a blast of blinding pain. This was no rope; it was the cord of the percolator filled with hot coffee that poured over my head and shoulders. I screamed. The pain, blinding as it was only lasted for a few moments when the angels came and took me out of my body.

There was no way to cope or understand what had happened to me, and I suspect this is why the angels came and were present in the hospital. I was covered from head to toe in gauze while everyone wondered if I would live or die. The pain returned, and I was crying, no, I was bawling uncontrollably on the pillows. I realized it was not my pain that I was feeling but my mother's! It was very sad because I was alright, but my mother was overwhelmed with guilt.

I returned to the pillows and breath work many times as session after session took me back to where I could see and feel past events. My mother was never able to release the feeling of guilt. I was able to do the breath work, to re-experience and release old feelings like particles trapped in the fabric of my being. The emotional turbulence I feared, and the defensive life jacket I wore for protection, began to disintegrate.

As I read these lines later, I find myself moving, going to another place inside. This was a place of feeling, a place intense with memories. These memories can be relived in the mind or in the emotions. Living only in the mind was getting old, and I wanted the company of my other part—who is she? How much do I know about my inner lady? Perhaps it is not necessary to know today? She knows me and I can trust that.

I became aware of the female nature within myself. Not in word or belief but in a place of knowing where feelings are communicated and the mind simply bears witness. Inner conflict dissolved as I realized She feels and pours love on all. In my own experience I know the mind of "man" can deny the sacred feminine within us with an overriding mental facility. He can go into the "I don't feel anything mode," at the drop of a hat. He was trained at a young age not to be like a girl. The culture does not encourage sensitivity in a man and getting a man to cry is not easy.

Those who are unable to feel the sacred feminine lack connection with the female side of themselves. I believe it is the fire mind of mankind that keeps the sacred feminine from manifesting on the world stage. These minds burn hot, and the water aspect of their beings are frozen solid.

This is the world we are presently leaving behind because the sacred feminine has not been welcome. Yet She is within all, surrounding the mind with her sensitive presence. If you love, she is present. It is always our choice to feel that which the mind of men has denied.

All that we feel is revealed in the field around us, there is no shadow in true light. In other words, the fire mind creates shadows that the sacred feminine reveals. It is as simple as that. Getting caught red handed by mother is one thing. Awakening to the fact that she can recall everything we did and felt from birth is a life-changing realization. We are more than just man or woman in physical bodies; we are the sacred feminine and masculine intertwined.

Spiritual Practice

Developing a spiritual practice means creating a personal "space" where we can retreat from the fast pace and ups and downs of our worldly life and have beneficial alone time. Daily meditation, yoga, or walking, something that benefits the body and mind and brings joy, better health, calmer mind, and emotions, all in balance with our age and ability. We give time to a personal practice in the same way we might give time to listen to the news, watch our favorite TV show, or drink a beer or glass of wine with friends. We can find a half hour in our day and make a commitment to at least sit comfortably and ponder.

A spiritual practice is like learning to read an old-fashioned directional compass to find a destination. We look at the dial to get the general direction. We put the compass back in our pack and start walking until we need the compass again. Having a sense that we are moving in right direction doesn't always mean it will be the easiest path. It's an important lesson to experience the feeling of the canyon walls closing in as the water in the river increases its speed. Sometimes an event grabs our attention. Rivers run calm and smooth or rage, depending on the flow of water, or in this case, the flow of thoughts and emotions.

A powerful example might be getting the news that your spouse has Stage 4 cancer. What name would we give that river canyon? The older ones die as the new ones are born. This is the way it is, for billions of years. Physical life is born, grows and dies--one more day in God's school.

A spiritual practice brings attention to our inner stability and builds awareness that we are moving deeper into our expanding consciousness. Nothing remains the same for long. Life is filled with movement on all three levels, and all three are equally a part of us. The physical body is our transportation vehicle in this world, and just like a bike or a car, they run for a while. Some run longer or shorter, yet eventually, they all stop. The question is, who are we when we no longer have a physical body? This prompts us to seek answers.

A spiritual practice is the beginning of taking charge of the unknown factor. A spiritual path is not necessarily a belief structure. Of course there are guidelines. Some people need a lot of guidelines when they first step foot on the path, others not as much. The path can become narrow, and we need to be balanced to walk it. It means we must do a lot of internal work/practice and then remain balanced as the wheel of life turns.

Seek and we shall find a way. That doesn't mean we avoid dealing with our "shit" on all its levels. It simply means we are moving along our lifeline and attempting to expand our consciousness, knowing one day we will no longer have a physical body.

We are all part of the whole. The old saying "humanity is one spirit" is a hint to where we will eventually arrive. The saying, "on earth as it is in heaven" is speaking to the individual soul who has ears to hear, preparing the person to understand the inner voice of our soul. In the "practice" we take time to tune into the deeper part of ourselves and tune into the vision and voice of our eternal soul.

Vision Quest

Native ways require some form of sacrifice. A vision quest requires four days of solitude with only a blanket/tarp, drum, fire, and water--no food or knife. This creates a unique situation where we can face ourselves without the normal daily distractions that fill our time and occupy our attention. After a day or two hunger is no longer an issue. It is the wild mind dealing coping without distractions. No phone, no food, or TV, just being with yourself in nature, like monks who go into The Cave.

Imagine seeing the effects that our thoughts, spoken words, or emotions have upon the environment. Our physical eyes are limited to seeing 10.15 Hertz while our technology can see the frequencies from 10.24 Hertz to 10.0 Hertz. We see only a fraction of the multidimensional world that exists around and within us. Our world is not all solid. Our bodies live in a world of density while our thoughts and feeling natures are not dense. They are free to do as we please or direct.

Learning to navigate our way through the distractions that occupy our attention in the physical, mental, and emotional worlds is the path to soul presence. We need to leave room for inner contemplation and conversations about unresolved inner confrontations that can only be avoided for so long. Being overly distracted avoids dealing with the inner voice. Daily meditation for thousands of days in a row builds an inner foundation. It helps to have friends who support your courage to make changes.

Vision Quest
April 1996

The week I wanted to do the vision quest opened up. Work and life were busy before and after. My friend Bernie offered to be at base camp and drop off water once a day. We established a place for the drop off on the way in. I had a blanket, sleeping bag, tarp, drum, tobacco, walking stick, water, and a hat—that's it.

We arrived at base camp mid-morning. From there it was half hour walk to the base of the rim of the High Mesa. I hiked to the top of the ridge and headed northwest. As I walked, I silently asked my power animal to lead me to the right spot. I arrived at a place with two boulders facing South. They were about 4 feet high, 6 or 8 feet long, and 6 feet wide, with a small gap between them. I leaned my pack against one of the rocks. To the West was a juniper tree with a flat rock beneath. The North was open and to the East about 30 feet away was another juniper tree.

After I laid my pack down, I walked around to see and feel if there was another spot where I should be. There wasn't. When I came back, Bernie was 30 feet to the West, sitting on a rock that could be used as a tub if it rained enough. We lit sage, hugged, and he walked away.

It was still morning and getting warm when the wind started to blow. I laid my blanket in the shade of the tree and rested. When I got up it was still warm. I took off my clothes, except for the moccasins, and built a circle. I started with the four directions and filled in the rest until the circle felt complete. In the center, I made a circle for a fire. I gathered wood and set my blanket in place between the fire and the South.

Later, at sunset I lit the fire and smudged myself, my drum, the circle, and a larger circle around the rocks and trees. I came back to the blanket and drummed for a short time, asking for guidance. I was tired, so I laid down and gazed at the moon and stars. During the night I would often wake up and place a few more sticks on the fire. The wind was gentle and steady from the southwest. At some point it stopped, then turned and came from the north. The air was colder, and then the clouds came.

When I saw the first hint of dawn, I let the fire go out. When the first rays of the Sun hit my face, I woke up completely. I felt weak when I got up. I leaned on a rock or laid down on another. I realized that I had nothing to do. No coffee to make or food to eat. No one to call or any place to go. I would lean on a rock and drift off to no place, or think I still had three more days.

I took a walk to the ridge, which was a few 100 yards to the South, thinking I could climb down and get out of the wind, which worked to some degree. Then I started to feel small pains in the bottom of my stomach and intestines. I assumed it was hunger and tried not to think about it. The body had a loud voice, and I started to hear a story I once read where a grandma was telling the grandson about the body mind and the spirit mind. My body mind was getting very loud.

The wind became strong, and I could feel it start to bite under my pullover. I walked and looked under the juniper trees for incense. When I found one, I would crawl under the tree and pick it off the ground. When I had collected all I could find, my situation would come pouring back into my awareness.

When I got back, I put on my jacket and laid on the blanket. The wind was strong and there was no comfort. I got up and went to the tub to lie down, hoping it would stop the wind--it didn't. I went back to the circle, put the blanket down, and got in my sleeping bag. I pulled it over my head and warmed up. I stayed in that position for what must have been hours.

About three hours before the sun would go down,

I needed to drop off an empty water bottle so Bernie would know I was okay. I walked to the spot, and it felt good to see he had left three full bottles. I gave silent thanks to my friend.

After I returned with the water, I had to deal with the wind. I pulled some logs over and tried to make a wind block on the north side of the circle, which turned out to be useless. Even worse, it created a loud noise with the tarp and sprayed dirt in my face.

At that point I realized I couldn't sleep in the inner circle. Maybe I could make a shelter between the South rock and the West tree. I wished for a tent and cursed out loud at the cold wind. The north sky looked black, threatening a cold rain or snow that didn't look far off. I worked and struggled to make a shelter because it was still inside the outer circle I had created. I thought it might work if I could just block the wind a little more.

Close by, leaning on the West side of the South rock, was a slab of rock that I thought might do the job. I moved the rock about six inches when a brown pack rat about the size of a hamster and it's three babies looked back at me. Everyone ran except one who was the size and color of a regular mouse with big ears. That rodent stayed and looked back at me. I felt like an intruder in their home and gently put the rock back.

The sun was setting, and my vision quest had become a matter of survival. I went to a boulder a few yards to the southeast and discovered the wind did not blow on the south side. I built a fire with the coal from the circle and managed to make a lean-to with my tarp.

I put my drum, blanket, and sleeping bag inside and carried wood over for the fire. I crawled inside and the warmth and comfort of the rock and the fire was great. It was a pleasure, and I gave thanks. I slept and kept the fire going.

In the morning, when the sun was still low, I crawled out of the shelter, still feeling weak. The day was clear and cool. I had nowhere to go and nothing to do but exist. I felt drunk when I tried to walk. I was grateful I had a walking stick to lean on. I went from rock to rock and just laid down or rested standing up. The pain had stopped, and hunger was not the issue. The issue was keeping my mind from wandering and wondering when this would be over.

I didn't stay up for long, I was just too weak. I laid back down in the shelter and my body ached. I wanted to curl up and sleep, but sleep would not come. I had visions of starving people curled up like this with their big eyes looking at me. I thought of the people I've seen with AIDS who had a hard time walking twenty feet. I began to experience a separation of my body and mind. I could find comfort outside of the body. There is a place to go. I am not just a body, which I always knew. That experience made it real.

Near noon I felt strong enough to take a walk, but the walk did not last long. The wind was still cool, and I was having a mental battle. How nice it would be to have soup when I got back to camp. I was glad I had told a few people I was going to stay for four days. It gave me strength. *I can do this.*

I went back to the shelter. The sun seemed to stop its motion. I would doze off and think time went by. I would look at the Sun through the tarp, but the yellow orb did not seem to move. It became a waiting game. I was not worried about having a vision, how could I when I was struggling so much?

Some time that afternoon I decided to make friends with the wind. I asked the wind to please take away these thoughts of the past and future and bring a vision on the wind.

I was still in the shelter when the sun was just past the middle of the afternoon. I needed to drop off empty water bottles for the day so Bernie would know I was alright. I had an urge to roll some tobacco in a cigarette and smoke it. I did take at least a few shallow puffs. I got up, put the water bottle and leather bag over my shoulder, and walked to the drop off place. Bernie had dropped off another bottle that I really didn't need, but I took it. Looking down at base camp only caused pain because the future fantasy was fruitless. I still had two more nights.

When I was back at the circle I was still unsure if the weather would allow me to spend the night inside the circle. I gathered fire wood and just before the sun set I lit the fire and carried my blanket and sleeping bag to its place on the south side.

I sat and drummed with the fire burning, and for the first time I sang and the song came from a very deep place. I sang to the wind, "Oh wind, carry my vision. Take away the past and future." I was physically unable to stay in a good posture for long. I laid down and gazed at the moon and stars.

That night I dreamed I was lying in a bed with a woman when I found myself becoming aroused the dream changed. I was out of the bed and in a dark hall, entering a larger room. Even though I couldn't see, that's what I felt. Then a woman appeared in front of me. She had a name of someone I once knew but she did not look like her. She was very tall and had large breasts that were at my face level. I was not aroused.

I began to hear a song from the late sixties, "Don't let the past remind you of what we are not now." I woke at that point and put a few more sticks on the fire.

When I woke on the fourth morning, it was clear and warmer. I still felt weak but better. My head was full of the woman from my dream. I reached out the the wind. The past is like yesterday's weather and has no place on this quest. I asked the wind to blow it away.

At midday I took a walk to the West. I wasn't far when I saw myself standing before a group of businessmen at a weekend workshop. I was talking about the value of taking time off and remembering how to have fun. I thought I can't do this. Then I heard, "If you can do four days, you can stand in front of businessmen and teach them something about fun."

This spontaneous vision was exciting because it came on its own and was the first thing that happened to me in that realm. Then it came to me that I should write and buy a laptop computer and take it wherever I went. I continued on my walk, feeling better than ever. I would lose myself under the juniper tree when I found one that had incense.

I came back to camp and rested. When the sun was low enough, I went to check on the water, and the full bottles were there. I imagined myself at the camp just below the hill. I could see the entrance to the Cove. I allowed myself to dream for a few moments as I burned some incense. The end was near, and I felt good. Vision or no vision, I was given plenty, and I was grateful.

When I was back at the circle, I began to pack and straighten up. It was the last night, and I didn't want the shelter to remain. When all was put away, I knew that this night I would spend it on the north side of the circle. I was ready before the Sun went down and started the fire. I used the large logs, and as they burned, I pushed them in.

I sat in a straight posture and felt the surge of energy. I took my shirt and moccasins off and drummed. As I felt the energy rise, I called out from a deep place within me and sang.

When I stopped, I still felt good, my back stayed straight, and I was not tired. I added a few more sticks to the fire. I was sitting when a wave that seemed to come from the West hit me. I felt the urge to cry. I whimpered a few times and went into my head. This emotion seemed to remain close.

I asked within myself to go with the experience. It

hit again, and I cried and cried. Then I began to cry out loud to open my heart. I peeled away at my chest to open my heart. I reached into the fire until my hands were hot and placed them on my chest. I did this many times. I was not worried about not having a vision. How could I when I was struggling so much.

Some time that afternoon, I decided to make friends with the wind. I asked the wind to please take away these thoughts of the past and future and bring a vision on the wind. I felt the urge to drum and journey to my guardian animal and ask if he might show me a vision.

We met in the Meadow and then I was on his back. I wanted to open my heart, and I pressed my chest against his neck, and it felt good. I asked if he could show me a vision. We went in a circle in the Meadow. Then we were in the Taos Valley, we were flying around the valley, over the mountains to the east and toward the West. We went around many times. When we stopped, we were in the South section of the Taos area. There is much in Taos to open to so the meadows should no longer be an issue. I saw a house with a greenhouse and an electric solar panel on the roof. I stopped drumming.

I felt good and I laid down, and when I woke in the morning, I felt good. I wondered if I would still feel good when I stood up. I did. I had a few hours left, so I lit the fire and started packing up. Then I took the Medicine Wheel apart and placed the rocks in a place where they felt they belonged. I still had a small stack of wood, and I knew when I was finished burning them Bernie would show up.

When the last fire burned out, I looked up and saw Bernie coming through the trees. We opened our arms to each other from a distance and I felt him. We smudged, and I placed the last of the sage on the coals. When it was finished, I poured the last of my water on the fire.

I felt strong enough to carry my pack as I walked to the southeast corner of the Ridge, and I followed Bernie down. I was once again glad I had a walking stick. When we were back at the camp, I felt blissful. I would just laugh. When I tasted the potato, corn, catfish, and dumpling stew, I could hardly contain my excitement and joy.

Medicine Wheel

The Medicine Wheel teachings have been around for thousands of years. It was love at first sight for me with the teachings because they were simple, clear, and deep. Deep is where we need to go to find our true self. The basic teachings can give us a vision that allows us to identify where we are in relationship to the entire wheel of our ever-turning life.

The general idea is to get all four directions healed and balanced and remain aware that we need to "maintain the balance," which is another reason why developing a daily practice is helpful. It's a healthy habit, like drinking enough water and brushing our teeth. When the four directions are in balance we become centered in our alignment with our soul and soul's purpose.

Like a wheel we can spin in or out of balance. Medicine wheels are great mirrors for our lives. Each direction holds another story. When the stories balance, we begin to live in the center. The medicine wheel teachings are practical because they shine light on an inward path that leads to our awakening and eventually living in of our center. We observe, we touch the physical world, and we emotionally feel the world around and within us. The path, any true path, leads to understanding our situation as a human born on Earth at the present time.

The Medicine Wheel has spokes, much like a bicycle wheel. If the spokes are out of tension with each other the odds are the wheel is going to wobble as we ride down the path. When we say, "I have to get my shit together!" we are recognizing a wobble. The medicine wheel (for this conversation) has four major directions and the center. We can assume that most people are not balanced or living in the center hub of their lives. From the center hub we can observe our life and learn to remain balanced. This means we won't freak out over something and allow it to make our bike difficult or impossible to ride. We all know that experience, so this is a work in progress.

Each direction reveals a place within us that we hadn't realized or awakened to. As we look at the four directions, we can begin to see how each direction on the wheel can affect the others. We are the "wheel," attempting and seeking to bring it into balance. Unless we are totally out of balance, we have a sense, or ability to ponder, where we are within the wheel, discovering where we might need more work to bring about a better balance.

The beauty of the Medicine Wheel path is it teaches not just with words and prayers, but with clear direction and guidance how to go within and experience first-hand what is true beyond belief. It teaches us through personal inner experience. We've all heard stories of monks, sages, and gurus who have gone off to live in a cave for extended periods. Solitude is something worth experiencing. Solitude without distractions is a powerful experience whether it is an hour a day, a week, or whatever you can manage. We are told that Jesus went into the desert for 40 days and nights.

SOUTH

In the south we find the trust of a child, our inner child. What does that mean? Trusting our action? Trusting our thinking or feeling? We learn that even though we are afraid or nervous, we can trust and move forward anyway. Without trust, fear takes over and stop us cold. Allowing ourselves to move into the unknown is a form of trust. We might feel a little or a lot nervous, yet we jump into the river current knowing we need to move on. Just because we are older doesn't mean that little child no longer exists. I love to play with my friends. We all have older bodies now and yet that child is still there. Jesus said, "only if you become as children can you enter the kingdom of God!"

In the south we learn to trust that we can handle the results of our actions on any of the three levels. We can learn to adjust to what works best for us individually. In the south, trust is a big simple word. The child knows trust. The baby trusts its mother's touch as it sleeps and get nourished. The question is, how does the trust of a newborn with its mother relate to an adult living and working in the world?

The south axis travels north to the mountains where we learn to walk the narrow path. A child comes into the world with no baggage and the warrior who climbs the mountain to his true self must release and let go of everything. It is on the mountain peak that one finds the true self. It is the place where we truly experience who we are without worldly attachments. We are souls, we go within and discover there really is another world that we can live in while on earth. "On earth as it is in heaven" comes from the Bible.

Its blissful in many ways and when the inner child is happy the soul warrior who faces the world is more balanced. The south is about trust, it is where our inner child lives. Have we protected and nurtured our inner child now that we adults? Or have we forgotten the little boy or girl? The soul can shine thru the eyes and heart of a child. We have all felt it. We've also experienced or witnessed the opposite, where the inner child is squashed or simply not allowed to happen or told, don't be a child!

NORTH

In the north, on the opposite side of the wheel, we learn how to be truly alone. The path to the north takes us into the mountains and solitude. At first, when we head in that direction, the path is wide, and we begin to see the white capped mountains in the distance. Slowly the path narrows and becomes steeper. We soon realize that if we want to proceed on the narrower steeper path, we need to unload some of the extra weight we are carrying on our back. What could this be? Perhaps it is a grudge we are still holding from years back in our life? The list goes on and on.

If we want to continue to the mountain top, everything must eventually be emptied out so we are totally naked, where nothing within us is hidden. Then we are at the top of the mountain and can look around without outside distractions. We can look at the north south axis and feel the balance that both bring to each other. The unconditional trust of the child brings the ability to let go of baggage. If we didn't have the trust to drop our internal baggage, we would lack the strength to walk the steep and narrow path.

EAST

East is about illumination and clarity of mind that transcends belief. In the east we manifest our dreams. The world of humans on the mental level is where we conceive our beliefs. Religious beliefs cover a very broad spectrum. I often use the Catholic belief/teaching I grew up with in the 50's and 60's as a simple example of why we eventually need to get beyond beliefs and catch a glimpse of reality. When I was growing up, prior to 1966, I was taught that eating a hamburger at a Friday night summer barbecue was a mortal sin, the equivalent of murder. This could land you in the eternal fires of hell unless you confessed to a priest behind the screened booth and did your penance before you died. Did anyone really believe that? The teachings of the Roman Catholic Church were so simplistic that I am stunned that people went along and never really questioned.

How do we get beyond belief? It's a good question. The easy answer is we need to get balanced. We need to start tuning our guitar strings. The closer we are to being in tune, the deeper we can go into the depths of understanding/vision/clarity—balance and harmony.

WEST

In the West we learn about dreams. We dream the dream that we can make real, while looking at our intention and using our clarity of mind. Can we make our dreams real? Do we dream dreams that are in harmony with humanity, the divine plan, and Mother Earth's best interest? We learn about our intuition and discernment when it comes to holding on to our dream. Remember the saying "the American dream?" In the 50's and 60's the dream was to go to school, get a job so when we retired at age 65, we no longer needed to work for money.

Today we are touching upon a much bigger dream to discover what we really want. Are we dreaming with clarity of mind, or are we dreaming with a mind that only wants material wealth? The center balance in the east and west accrues when the dreams are in harmony with clarity of mind.

Focus is one way to bring clarity of mind. An athlete focuses on fitness training that best supports the goals. A businessman might be focused on making millions of dollars. It's connected to internal Focus when it comes to developing clarity of mind. The list goes on and on because everyone has the free will to develop focus as they see fit. However, there are many warning signs on these roads that many a businessman fails to heed. They may burn bridges and destroy others' lives with little or no concern for the harm they caused. This can be on the world stage or within the confines of our small little world. Once we develop clarity of mind we have power. We have taken up the sword of life, and it is a double edge sword. One side serves the greater purpose of all concerned and the other serves only itself.

East and west are on the same axis. We can imagine how aligning the east west axis can be a very powerful force in the world for better or worse.

Ponder, it's like dreaming, but with a focused attention to explore, seeking understanding and clarity about the bigger picture while still taking care of the physical, emotional, and mental needs. One cannot say that there is only one path, or that one path is better than another. There are many true paths to our soul, and it is our free will to seek and find what works best for us individually.

"Store not your treasures on earth" (Matthew 6: 19-21) speaks directly to this. We must take into our perspective that we can't take anything with us when we leave this physical world other than the love and wisdom we have gained. We are souls, we can go within and discover there really is another world that we can live in while on earth. As in Matthew 6: 10 where Jesus says, "Thy will be done on earth as it is in heaven."

To find one's true self, the part of us that doesn't change like the wind, we must find our center. After a while we need to learn how to stay centered. Again, this is a good reason to develop a practice and habits to take time to do something healthy. When we take time for ourselves in the balanced, healthy, spiritual, esoteric, physical, mental, and emotional way, we bring the kingdom of heaven to earth. It is within us, which also manifests materially in the physical world. Imagine what it will take to bring peace on earth.

The idea that Jesus will soon return and save us needs to be grounded in the reality of the present world situation. Imagine what human consciousness work must be accomplished before the Christ can have a presence on earth big enough to be heard around the world. Remember that the last time Christ took physical form the world population was only 300 million. And now it 8 plus billion and climbing.

Christ, as the world leader, will not appear externally until humanity sets the stage for His return. Christ's basic teaching is "to love everyone including your enemy." To love everyone is required at some point if we seek higher expansive soul consciousness. It is the kingdom within. Any way is the right way so long as you are growing in Love.

Of course, there needs to be preparation for the return of the Christ, which is one of the reasons we need to develop a daily practice. We need to get in shape to explore and discover for ourselves what works and what doesn't. There is such a wide range of human beings and there are many paths that lead to our true self, our soul. It's not unusual to explore different paths in our search. It's a bit like starting college in liberal arts because we are not sure where we want to go with the college experience. We search for something that might grab our interest and focus as we remain open to new ideas.

There are many trials and lessons as we adjust to what works better or best at any given time. We might find something that works perfectly for now only to be replaced tomorrow, next week, next month, or year. We strive to get all four directions on the Medicine Wheel balanced and to remain aware that we need to maintain the balance. This is another reason for developing a daily practice, like drinking enough water, and brushing our teeth.

Earlier, when the population of Earth was in the millions instead of billions, a spiritually inclined person, generally a man then, might find himself in a monastery with varying degrees of solitude for his entire life. This is no longer possible in the West. It was the old way when the human population was much smaller and communication between people was face to face. We are now in the age of Aquarius, and everything is different. The old way is fading, and we are adjusting to the huge increase in population and technology. Earlier ways of ruling people with violence are coming to an end.

Time only exists in the physical realm because here everything is temporary. Our spiritual work is to develop a consciousness where we begin to see from the higher self-perspective. Call it tuning into our eternal soul, which is the part of us that is not connected to time. The soul watches the ego personality not only from birth to death, but from lifetime to lifetime. It's like a parent watching a baby grow from birth to adulthood. For the soul, each physical life is one day in God's school.

The Inner Child

We need to develop a relationship with our inner child. When we become a warrior, we protect our inner child. Eventually, if we are to be healthy people, we will develop oneness with our inner child (and all children). One key to our personal stability is directly connected to our relationship between our adult self and the child within.

We begin to see that we are all here together. My God and your God has nothing to do with it. This is not the time to get into political and religious arguments. A limited few control the masses, but how can we find and maintain our internal stability while our present cultural foundation starts to dissolve. The child in me says we need to learn to learn how to "play more better," quote from the *Guardians of Recreation* videos.

A Time of Great Change

Perfect circumstances for growth are always present when we trust and respond in gratitude for all that is given. There are no accidents in a world where we reap what we sow, where energy follows thought, and for every action there is a reaction. Avoidance of this reality may be reflected in the human law that gives power and limited liability to the nonhuman entity of the corporation. But there can be no avoidance without a future confrontation. Simply said, the distraction of the material world allows us to avoid who we are on the deeper levels.

We must grasp the reality behind the words "humanity is one spirit" and realize that the child within is as important as the adult who faces the world.

One day everything came to an abrupt halt when I was no longer required to attend school. The prospects of taking on a full time job for the next 40 years didn't sit well. The happiness I felt as a kid started to evaporate.

I was lost and searching for something or someone to explain what was happening. I wasn't buying the 40 years of full-time work (starting now) and "no heaven until you die" version of life. I started asking everyone around me "What is going on?" Why are we alive? What are we here to do?" No one had answers and most became uncomfortable with my line of questioning.

Like the snap of a finger, childhood playmates

were disappearing from the banks of the river where we played. They took the bait and were being reeled inland to the mass consuming culture with only two weeks' vacation a year. It freaked me out to think I could be reeled in like that. I turned and walked into the river, deeper and deeper, until the current pulled my feet off the bottom. It was here in the river that I started to feel like a child born into a new world. All was pleasurable until the river picked up speed. With no feet on the ground my thoughts were running wild.

I felt like I was losing myself and reached out to the cosmos for help. Books started to appear, and I soon discovered that what I was feeling was not unusual. I felt like Jonathon Livingston Seagull when he first left the flock in Richard Bach's story of the same name. Then, with no attraction to religion I read the Bible and discovered Jesus was not talking about religion he was talking about a way to live life. I was introduced to his simple version of karma when he said, "you reap what you sow." I felt an attraction to the concept that if we "seek the kingdom within ourselves first all else shall be given." At the time, I was seeking internal answers and took the "given" as a good sign to continue letting the river take me down stream. I was never hungry or without comfortable shelter from that day on.

Time

The shift from dark to light as the ages change simply means people are awakening to the reality that we are all here together. Our ability to remain in balance as situations around us change will become the norm. How we reach that place of balance in the meantime is our purpose, our yoga, our work, our spiritual path. At some point the conscious majority will govern and exclaim, the purpose for living is to find joy and expand our consciousness for the benefit of all. We must want goodness for all, simple as that. As we find our center, we help the world find its center, but it will take some time.

The distractions of the material world cause us to avoid who we are on a deeper level. As people we are played like puppets on a string and are subject to the waves of the economy and world affairs. We can realize that perfect circumstances for growth are always present when we trust and respond in gratitude for all that is. This is how we build the strength to hold our inner stability. The basic rules are simple and easy. We've must desire and act for the goodness of all. To wish, or to do otherwise, creates separation, pain, and confusion.

Spending time dreaming dreams that we can manifest is empowering. The manifested power can be black white or shades of gray. It makes sense that we reap what we sow. This holds true everywhere our presence makes its imprint. The physical mental and emotional environments are the playing fields.

SATURDAY
LAST QUARTER — THE KINGDOM OF GOD

Today is a Saturday, that doesn't mean that much anymore. It's not like it was when we were growing up or during the years of full-time work and raising kids.

Sometimes I think Wednesday is a Saturday. Without the rhythm of a work a day week, or some other daily or weekly rhythm that requires our attention, like a job and a family life. The time clock acts in a different way when we are no longer ruled by the clock.

We are entering into a new or different reality. We played for the first 5-7 years, then we were in school for the next 12-16 years as our play time was cut way down. At 18 we finished high school, we had three options, enter the work force, go to college, or join the military. After experiencing all that, we are now retired from the 40-hour week paycheck.

In the morning, meditation is first, then a nice cup

of coffee while I check to see if there are any friends to communicate with, check the headlines that suggest we humans have some work to do before we can bring the Kingdom of Heaven on Earth, finish the coffee, and the day starts.

Tuesdays, I play music with my friends, Thursdays I attend a small men's group. I like to ride my bike in the afternoon along a winding dirt path in the trees by the river.

Once we retire, what's next? Will something new grab our attention? How will we fill the time gap that was created? Think about all the time we spent doing stuff for our career and then add in the travel time between home and work, our marriage, finances and children?

What are we doing within ourselves when we sit comfortably with no visual or sound distractions that grab our eyes and ears for attention? One thing that happens is our conscious thoughts, imagination, and emotional feeling nature are set free from the attention of the physical body.

We've heard stories of monks in the past going off into a cave or monastery for months or years. Jesus went into the desert for 40 days and 40 nights to experience solitude. When he returned, he was ready to allow the Christ to use his physical vehicle to complete his work. Then the Christ lifted Jesus off on the cross when he asked, "Why has thou forsaken me?" So, the story goes.

The trick about solitude and why it is a challenging

experience, has to do with our lack of alone time with nothing to do but sit and be with oneself. If we were able to strip away everything that is going on inside our head, and all our emotional waves came to a calm, where would we be?

We are at the door to the inner reality of who/what we are when we remove the physical from the picture. We are a soul having a human experience. Our eventual goal is to bring our soul consciousness into the physical reality. That is how we create the reality of The Kingdom of God on Earth as it is in Heaven.

Life Purpose

Humans have created or discovered many different pathways, both outward and inward. A spiritual path is about discovering my Path, realizing that one day our life will be over. We can't take anything physical with us when we pass and find ourselves on the "other side" without a physical vehicle. Money, cars, and the cost of housing no longer exist. All our focus on survival needs, goals, and money no longer hold value. Imagine if you get to the other side and have zero understanding of what the fuck is going on? All you had lived for and focused on was suddenly meaningless and unattainable now that you no longer have a physical body in this dimension.

Many find themselves on the other side still attached to thoughts of money-power and control over others that were motivating factors while they lived in the physical vibrational plane. Like attracts like, and when it comes to what we hold on to within ourselves, we discover that is what creates our vibration. We were told to seek within first. This is also connected to the teachings around attachment. We still take our emotions and mental attachments with us. Then we realize why the teachings of Christ to love everyone, including our enemies, is such a powerful teaching.

If we take the physical body out of the picture and place our consciousness in the eternity of our reality, which is as the Christ said, "within you," our unknown perspective of our true reality in consciousness will gradually awaken and we will begin to realize.

Angels, gods, saints, gurus, and teachers are here to help us. They teach and guide us, showing how the game works. Christ's teaching to love everyone is the keynote, especially now. If we are disturbed, then there is a need, a lesson, or a test of our ability. Yes, sometimes we are overwhelmed. We learn to slow the thought process, learn to still the mind--no thoughts, just awareness as we become more centered. When thoughts slow down, or stop, and the heart feels love, the door begins to open. What are we doing daily, or often, to bring our self into balance and alignment?

We seek a calm mind and a loving heart. What could be better? Of course, this is easier said than done. It's a lifelong discipline with a learning curve. Everyone is different and finding a path that fits our needs both internally and externally is what the searching is all about. Jesus said, "The Kingdom of

God is within you." (Luke17:21). He didn't say the Kingdom of God is only in Heaven. He also said, "The Kingdom of Heaven is at hand." (Matthew: 4:17).

Perhaps as we ponder it becomes easier to grasp reincarnation with the view that each life is like one day in God's school. Our work is to bring the Kingdom of God on "Earth as it is in Heaven." If we seek the kingdom, we will eventually find it. We are on the path, we are conscious, and we are learning and becoming more aware of the Eternal even though we live in time. Our work is to bring the eternal consciousness into our conscious awareness.

There is something for everyone when we seek. If we are not seeking, then what are we doing? You could be a mother of four little kids and a busy lady in the human world, At this moment, this is your path, but you need to take care of yourself.

Once I told my guru, "I am so busy with my construction business, and my wife and daughters, I can't get up at 4 am to meditate." He looked at me and said, "Your work is now your Yoga." Our Practice is how we live our life. The essence of the teaching and of the practice was to become a channel for Christ light and love and try to walk thru daily life with a calm mind and a loving heart. Walking the inward path is a difficult challenge in present conditions since the culture doesn't focus on serving humanity.

I laugh, now, because at thirty-five my entire being was ramped up. This was the beginning of a lifelong yoga practice. The word yoga is derived from the Sanskrit root *Yuj*, meaning "to join" or "unite." Yogic scriptures teach that the practice of Yoga leads to the union of individual consciousness with that of universal consciousness, indicating a perfect harmony between the mind and body, man & nature.

Super Rich

The Super rich earned their billions through the labors of humanity, Earth's resources, and well planned government leaders who bend the rules in favor of corporations. We have come to a place where corporations have the power to influence our destiny. Remember, corporations do not have souls.

Puppet leaders and workers are an endless supply as a corporate friend once said, "They will pay for as much of your soul as you are willing to sell." We are a planet full of human souls and know deep within ourselves that we are responsible for our actions. The Bible tells us, "You reap what you sow." Some of us thought we were so smart that we had figured out a way to get around being responsible for our actions. The corporation was created to insulate the owners from personal liability, so we've created an entity with no soul and given it power to influence the course of our destiny. Drill baby, drill .

Let's start another war. We've been warned about the problems and difficulties of a rich man getting into heaven, but this is not about religion. This is about a few winning the game of monopoly and refusing to start a new game. The transition into adulthood can be tricky business. At what point in our life do we think it is appropriate to be a balanced and healthy human? Although there are exceptions, corporations are generally soulless entities that are not obligated to give back. They can make billions or trillions and hoard it from the people.

I would propose that soulless corporations would not be allowed to hoard the wealth. We should look at the health of our world, and then ask, "Are the ones with all the money acting in the best interest of all of us, or just in the interest of corporate profits?" I think we went wrong when we created the law to limit one's liability behind the protection of corporate shield. This gives individual human souls the false illusion that they are not responsible for directing the ship of the mass corporation. What did Jesus say to this? "You reap what you sow." There is no doubt that wealth needs to be redistributed--it is a board game that many of us are losing.

Part Two

"One who previously has made bad karma, but who reforms and now creates good karma, brightens the world like the Moon appearing from behind a cloud."

The Buddha

Lessons from Life's Journey

Much has been written about Near Death Experiences, NDEs, where a person disconnects from the physical for a time and later returns to waking consciousness to tell their story. And yet, we remain conscious, it's like playing a character in a play and then returning to our own identity. The key is to spend time and focused effort to get in touch with the part of us that survives, so when we get to the other side we are not bewildered.

When we depart this life, we take nothing with us but our love, wisdom, and karma. If haven't learned to seek love and wisdom in life and instead have focused only on the material world and ignored the reality within, circumstances when crossing over might be different. We take our consciousness, our "essence," because we are no longer attached to a physical body.

Two of the world's greatest teachers, the Christ, and the Buddha, gave clear messages that we as individual souls are responsible for our actions. We reap what we sow (karma) on all the levels. Understanding the basics of God/Great Spirit's creation is to realize there are consequences for our behavior and choices. Our experience here on earth is not a one-time gig, we return to physical embodiment over and over.

Perhaps that is why we received the teaching, "Seek first the kingdom of God and all else shall be added," (Matthew 6:33) and "Do not store up for yourselves treasures on earth, where moths and vermin destroy, and where thieves break in and steal. But store up for yourselves treasures in heaven." (Matthew 6: 19-21). Or, as the Buddha taught, "The root of suffering is attachment."

Knowledge of universal laws that govern our lives is like a handy flashlight on the path. Do we seek the kingdom within while living and working in the world? There are rules governing our actions as a soul occupying a human body

Leaders need to give their followers the information and guidance necessary to eventually move on and follow his or her own way. Teachers can point the way and give good instructions, but eventually we need to take responsibility. We need to find out what works by experimenting. We must learn about the speed of our pace and feel comfortable going fast or slow and everything thing in-between.

We are all occupied with our thoughts and emotions to a greater or lesser degree. We have all been overrun with internal struggles at some point. This is not our physical brain, it is our mental and emotional bodies thinking and feeling that then filters down into the physical and the personality acts it out. The personality can have many different beliefs as also reflected on our present world stage.

Cycles

Everything in the Universe spins and Earth is likewise in constant motion. On the other side, there is no time. We have time here because physical life is limited. From an astrological perspective, each year we move through all twelve zodiac signs as Earth orbits the Sun. On a much larger scale, due to Earth's wobble, a cycle called precession of the equinoxes takes approximately 26,000 years. The twelve divisions of that cycle are the astrological ages. And on an even grander scale, our Solar System orbits the Milky Way galaxy on a journey that takes 250,000 years.

We can look back through human history and see changes that have taken place as the ages changed. Christ came two thousand years ago at the beginning of the Age of Pisces. Two thousand years before in the Age of Aries, Moses walked the Earth when symbolic gods were rams. As the age changed from Aries to

Pisces, the Lamb of God gave way to the Fisher of Men. Before that in the age of Taurus there were sacred cows and bulls. Now we are at the beginning of the age of Aquarius, the Water Bearer, and it seems that water and energy will increasingly become symbols of this age.

Imagine a racetrack that takes 26,000 years to go around. We are just entering a segment of the track that is a 2000-year curve. We can feel the intensity building as we hold on to the steering wheel of a car rounding the bend at 75 miles per hour. Or in the case of Earth, we hurtle through space at a speed of 67,000 miles an hour. If we don't pay attention to the details of our individual and collective action, we could easily lose control of our vehicle.

Feeling and discovering where we are in that current of life is a good start. It's from that place (within) that we can begin our search, doing something for our inner true self. It is the result of following Christ's teaching. We must learn to go beyond beliefs and find the reality behind the thoughts and emotions/feelings. We can test our beliefs and discover if they take us to a deeper reality or not. This is seeking our treasures in heaven. While we seek and we continue to survive in this world.

It's a form of discipline that's for our own good. In a world that is agitated and moving fast, our saving grace is taking time for ourselves to sit and be without phones or distractions. Take a walk, sit, learn how to meditate. Paint, do yoga, listen to inspiring music. It must be your time and no one else's. It is only when we slow down physically and internally that we begin to discover what's really happening in the moment. What are we thinking about? Where is our mental and emotional attention?

Balance Through Alignment
One Day in God's School Is a Lifetime

"Quiet the mind and the Soul will speak." The Buddha

Over the summer of 2020 I took time to express the concept that we have three separate yet intertwined bodies: physical, emotional, and mental. Upon physical death we continue to occupy the other two. We also have an eternal soul body that vibrates on a higher level. This is our true eternal self, waiting for the day when the three lower bodies align themselves in clarity, love, and light. The Soul can then fully enter the human vessel, embodying as Christ said, "On Earth as it is in Heaven." It's about raising our consciousness to grasp our place in the great unknown--the trick is to get our priorities in order.

Each human soul has three "bodies," physical, emotional, and mental. When we view ourselves from the energetic perspective of vibration, each of these bodies vibrates at a different frequency. Our job, work, or eventual purpose is to align and tune them like playing three keys on a piano or strings on a guitar. We can make a harmonious sound, or we can create a discordant sound that does not feel or sound good. We have been given instruments (our three bodies) and we need to figure out how to play them in tune.

Our connection with our eternal soul is the next level above or inward of our three lower bodies. The soul is like a singer in a band, using the musicians to express a message. In other words, our lower bodies are the band, and once we get the band to play in tune, the soul singer has a communication channel to these realms or frequencies.

We inhabit a physical body, using fingers to type words, eyes to see the road we drive on, and the list goes on. Emotions are feelings and feelings are vibrations of energy we feel and sense. We can feel love, calmness, peace, joy, or feel the frightening energy of fear and everything in between. Mentally, we can witness our experiences and remain calm as the river of life speeds up, or loose it completely in wild thoughts fed with uncertainty and fear of the unknown. The shifting currents of the river of life carries all of us along.

We vibrate on the mental, emotional, and physical planes. The mental plane holds our thoughts. Imagine you've been living in the dark and ever so slowly light has entered the physical world. That's like a thought that dawns on you. When the light dawns, you see something more clearly. The light of clarity of mind penetrates the clouds of unknowing, and you see in the mind's eye, a clarity beyond doubt, that you are heading in a good inward direction.

One way or another we are on the road, living a life in a physical body while also having an awareness of our thoughts in the thinking mind and feeling emotions that are usually connected to our thought process. Both affect the physical body and feeling physically "funky" can affect how we feel emotionally and mentally. It's all connected, and we are responsible for the thoughts and emotions we hold onto. The key words are "hold onto." Attachment is a source of suffering and hinders spiritual growth, as the Buddha taught.

When someone is experiencing a horrible situation, the feelings are so strong that fear can be triggered as the mind experiences a storm--tears, shaking, or loss. The opposite of that is feeling calm, love, and joy. It's the difference between floating on a calm clear lake in perfect weather, or in a wild windstorm while sitting in a small boat in the middle of the lake. This reminds me of Jesus walking on water or calming a storm.

This strong "feeling" is our emotional body. In the middle of that feeling, we may start to hear our thoughts. Do our thoughts speak wisdom, or run wild? Perhaps it is a combination. Thoughts can feed the emotional storm or bring the chaos down to a calmer more manageable level. The mental body is consciousness, our inner vision, and the higher level of the three bodies. It is where we dream our dreams during the day and talk to ourselves.

Our purpose is to expand our consciousness through repeated experiences to align all three aspects of our Being. The inward motivation is rewarded with a more expansive consciousness. When our three bodies start aligning, the eternal soul presents an opportunity to influence our lower three bodies, and we start our inward journey to the Great Spirit.

The reincarnating physical body experience is like an animal shedding its coats at the end of the season in preparation for the new one. We are still the same person with another life under our belt and another one on the way when the time is right. When we die, we find ourselves on the inner plane. The physical game is over, and if we are capable and ready, a life review takes place, and a plan is made for the next possible life.

Everything we do in our life has been recorded, and it is certainly a big surprise to many who never gave the afterlife a thought while they were cheating and abusing others for money and false power. It's all for naught when such people finds themself in the afterlife with a gang of people who all did a similar thing in their last lives. It is a form of hell. There is always a way out if one looks up and reaches for the helping hand with an inward recognition that we need help.

What does "going within" mean? Imagine going to a remote place, no Internet, books, pen, or paper.

There is just water, a blanket, and a tarp if shelter is needed. We can build a fire and maybe play a hand drum or a wooden flute--that's it. What happens when we have nothing to do but to be with ourselves? If we open to the experience, we can get to know the other parts of ourselves.

I can flash back to times when my thought mind was racing at full tilt, and emotional waves were up and down every few days. It was this crazy speed within myself that awakened a part of me to seek ways to calm down. Then one day, a few months or years pass, and you stop and reflect. You realize you have finally let go to a certain degree and realize you've come a long way. And yet, you realize it's only the beginning.

Free Will

With free will, we get choose. We've all seen the damage forced beliefs have upon a child or a country. We need to desire a greater understanding of how things work universally. We reap what we sow on all three levels. We are also in a world where someone can sow upon us something that we do not deserve and create karma for themselves. On the other hand, it could be a payback from several lifetimes ago. I think and believe this is why we are cautioned about the dangers of letting our consciousness go down the path of being judgmental.

All thoughts have vibration. Judgmental thought vibrations are quite different than the vibrational quality of kind, supportive, understanding, and loving thoughts and feelings. This is not to say that we become free from thinking judgmental thoughts, rather we learn not to hold on to them. They are like dark clouds passing in the sky, put enough of them together for an extended period and there will be a storm.

We attempt to slowly and gently find a way to stay in the center of the wheel of life where life stillness lives. Nothing changes yet everything changes because now we can see. We can perceive from the perspective of being balanced. From the center we interact, see, feel, play, and love, in all that life brings our way. It is our work to find the center, to discover where we are in relation to where we want to be.

Seek first and all else shall be given is part of the Christ's teachings, and this theme is also within the Medicine Wheel teachings. There are many true pathways back to our soul consciousness. We must discover how to live in the wild crazy world, walking the path at the same time. We must desire to expand our awareness, our understanding of how things are on all the levels while living and working in the world. The teachings can help point the way.

We work or have worked in the world to make money and survive. It's part of the human experience that forces us to interact with the world whether we like it or not. Now the work is to do our practice in our daily life and put it to the test. It is easy to stay calm when the atmosphere is calm. Can we remain calm with the World Wide Web, friends, family, children, grandchildren or spouse all asking for our attention? Can we remain, or work towards, always having a calm mind and loving heart? Is that not the ultimate purpose of being a human?

We are talking about getting in touch with our eternal soul, our true self. With soul contact we understand the relationship between our ego personality and our soul. This has everything to do with the Christ's teaching "to seek first the kingdom within and all else shall be given."

Dreams That Bring Goodness to All

As we roll along in the Universe, we always come back to the places and situations where our past experiences were not resolved. These reoccurrences are our responsibility to deal with and we must learn not to blame them on externals. Moving through and learning the lessons once and for all is how we come to our center. Being in our center does not mean that life and all its unexpected occurrences stop. Rather, it means we are centered within our being and are no longer thrown into chaos when the unexpected happens.

Our center can be described as the place where our mind is still and our emotions are calm. Like a ship on the sea, when the waters are calm we can see the horizon where the water meets the sky. We can feel the wind and see the ripples as the coming change makes its mark across the water. To still the mind and calm the emotions is the lifelong work since the average

American has never considered this. Our education prepared us to enter the workaday world.

During this educational process, we were hypnotized with advertisements by the alien world of the corporation through TV. This gave birth to the belief that we must work until 65, go into debt, eat fast food, buy material goods, and fight wars with other countries to feel safe, look good, and be happy. We watch TV until we fall asleep, or drink ourselves to numbness. This only prolongs the awakening process of dealing with who we are on the inside.

This appeared to work well for a time until the pollution of the planet and greed caused by materialism reached a crisis point that now endangers humans physically, mentally, and emotionally. As the wind creates ripples on the water, every action is imprinted. There is no way to get around the fundamentals of our universe--for every action there is a reaction. It is called the law of karma. It is the same law that Jesus refers to when he said we reap what we sow.

When women and men of the world stand up and say they will not allow our children to fight in wars, and when we no longer poison our children with junk food, TV, and plastic war toys, then we will be taking a major step in the right direction. The great divide among the people can be healed. The key is to practice what we know to be true. Every single one of us knows that the greatest power is love--to literally love our enemy and become harmless in all our actions is the simple answer. If we love, our perception of the world would change overnight and our dream to bring goodness to all would begin to manifest.

Reacting with compassion instead of anger the next time someone cuts you off on the highway, or the customer service person talks sharply to you on the phone, shifts the energy. If you act with love instead of anger, you will see how the waves within you bring calm as opposed to sending your entire being into a sea of rage.

The truth is, we really do reap what we sow. For every action mentally, emotionally, or physically, there is a reaction. Our response within ourselves and out into the world creates waves and energy fields. These waves touch others that are in the path. Karma, good or bad, is defined as the eventual result of our actions on ourselves and those within the range of repercussions of our actions. This is also the reason we cannot judge.

We must choose to love always, unconditionally, because repercussions spread until they eventually dissipate. This is why great prophets told us we must love our enemies and become harmless. It is the only way to calm the waters. I said above that our center is a place where our mind is still, and our emotions are calm. I need to add that our heart loves and repeat the mantra, "I love everyone without criticism. I am grateful for every experience."

Beliefs & Awareness

June 29, 2010

Many are happy to follow along with the program when material dreams are attainable, but it is quite a different story when we wake up from disillusionment of the material dream. This heaven can be whatever it is you wish it to be, but it must be within you and not outside of you if you wish it to last. Material riches can be pulled out from under our feet by outside forces such as wars and huge oil leaks.

It is not that adults revert to childhood to get into heaven, it is that the adult can access the child within. This is similar to having the ability to change hats, depending upon the situation. Losing contact with our inner child is the same as cutting off the roots to a tree. Yes, the adult can still function in the system, and the tree might have some use, but it will never again bear fruit.

It is not mind boggling when we realize that the ability to play in its true essence can heal our imbalances as an adult. Give cranky kids food and a nap, and they will play until they need more food and sleep.

In order to work, relationships take time. Play with friends is replaced with distractions. If we do not question the status quo, we simply follow along blindly. To understand that some people are willing to sell their souls to become rich should be enough to understand that heaven cannot be found within the system.

Finding Our Center

If we are having trouble being at peace or centered within ourselves, it may be wise to revisit our childhood and rediscover how and where we left our little boy or girl behind once we turned into adults.

The role of the child changes as we transition into adulthood, but it does not go away. The protection of mom's skirt from the harsh realities ultimately becomes our responsibility. How we protect, live, and play with our child as an adult speaks directly to our peace. Parents know happy children bring waves of peace to the family environment and are also very aware of the raging storms kids can bring into the house. As adults we all share the dilemma of figuring out how to live in this world and remain happy. This transition process is serious business and is a major development time of our life. A happy child within is required to be a healthy adult facing the outside world.

The transition to adulthood has a lot to do with

which part of the river you were in when you were cut free to fend for yourself. The wounded child acts out in multiple ways through the form of the adult. Our connection to the purity of our nature is directly linked to our child.

To trust is to understand that everything fits into place. To have clarity means that you see with a calm clear mind. It is a step beyond the thinking mind to a place of vision. If we cannot see clearly then how do we move forward? Life happens around where energy follows thought and action has repercussion.

As discussed in Chapter 17, Medicine wheels are great mirrors. Each direction holds another story of our life. When the stories balance out, we begin to live in our center. Granted we must start from the place of awakening wherever that may be. Commitment to face all the challenges that threaten to knock us out.

We can better face the outside world when we have a stable inner reality. Life still happens when we live in our center, the difference is we are no longer lopsided. They would have us believe that our center is directly related to the economy of our nation and world. There is some truth to that.

Once in our center, we go deeper into our self. It is the place where things become possible. Why? Because at that point we are consciously aware that everything is connected. It's a place of peace even in the middle of a great storm because we understand every situation is the perfect situation to test our skills.

Finding one's center is easy enough when we are in

a concentrated moment. Meditation, yoga, dance, sports and all the arts have the ability to bring us into balance. Remaining in our center when that moment passes is another matter. How do we hold our ground when waves wash over our heads and carry our thoughts and feelings out to sea, or when events wash over our entire being leaving us adrift in an endless sea with no land in sight?

What happens if you turn 19 and discover that you don't feel good. I mean up until that moment you enjoyed your life and suddenly you discover you feel pain and confusion on a mental and emotional level.

I felt lost and confused and clueless as to what was happening to me. All my religion and life experience to that point had left me flat. My dreams dissolved and I found myself in a reality that didn't correlate with what I had been told about life. There was more to it than getting a job and working to retirement. My religious education had strange rules like eating meat on Fridays was a mortal sin that held the penalty of eternal damnation.

I believe we are born into a wheel to continue our voyage. The first goal is to figure out how to keep the wheel from wobbling if we are looking for the center; then we must be willing to walk alone--go to places within oneself.

Becoming aware that we are subject to the nature of a spinning wheel helps us grasp what is happening to us while we are living on earth. It's not like we come here to a culture that is highly creative, balanced, and healthy. We are born into a world that seems to be at its wits end. The mass education of the populace is focused on material gain, earthly desire, and need of money. Between the polarities of right or left, there is a place of singularity where all humans are connected. But at this time on Earth, this place within us is not encouraged.

Mother and Me
An Internal Conversation

Many events shape a person'a life--the state of the world, state, town, family, parents, brothers, sisters, and the soul. Of all these, the soul is the main factor. Everything else has its influence, but the soul is who we really are. The soul has a thread to the all-encompassing Spirit of God.

We are here to learn a dance. We started out hungry and helpless and are put in the hands of someone who either wants us or doesn't. Did they want us so they could bring us through the early part of our lives with love, tenderness, strength, and wisdom? Or did our circumstance include all the possibilities from one end to the other? Somewhere in this new reality we begin to learn.

I am trapped, and when I feel this body upon my mother's breast, I feel secure. When I am away from it, I see shape and color. I touch and it is soft, and then one moment later it is different. I close my eyes to this strange place, and it is gone.

I lost my mother's breast after seven days. Things were not the same after that. The rubber nipple didn't feel as good, but it was all that was offered. They gave me what I needed, or I cried. Crying got me what I wanted. So, the first thing I learned about this world, "Ask and it shall be given."

I slept in a crib upstairs in the little room. There was a window I could look out once I was big enough to move around. There was a little baby painted on the side of the crib. The first experience that I consciously remember was my brother, or brothers, covered with a sheet, trying to scare me—it worked. I am glad that within a few seconds they realized this was not cool and took the sheet off and told me it was them.

Anything before that is a blur. The next memory is playing on the ground. I wore clothes and sat in the sun among the rocks, flowers, dirt, and grass. I was happy and loved to play more than anything, which was what I loved about being alive. It was an energy of a clear mind and calm emotions in the moment. We can still play after becoming adults and allow our play time to take us into that place of "no mind" joy.

———

A boy lived next door who was my size, maybe a little older, maybe he was 5 and I was 4. I know we, or he, knocked over and broke the bird bath. Somehow my parents blamed the boy. I know we were playing together, but if they wanted to blame him, I guess that was okay. I remember being told in some gentle way that he was not such a good boy, and it must have been his fault.

I don't remember feeling bad, and if I did, it wasn't for long. Maybe I felt bad for an hour or two, and for sure it was gone by the next morning. The issue never came up again until the rebirthing breath work experience when I was in my late 30's or early 40's.

As I write about this now, I realize that my mother was a little overprotective. She was fragile and needed calm emotions in the house. I was cute, nice, and smart enough to get away with doing kid stuff. My mother didn't need a troubled kid, and she figured out that I was happy on my own if I was playing and not making her worry.

As a child in school, I could read words, but I

didn't like reading and couldn't spell very well, which in turn, got me Fs and Ds on my report cards my entire school life. I remember once coming home with 5 Fs. I flash back now to how I cheated and never once got caught. I am 100% sure I would have gotten left back many times if I hadn't cheated. Believe me, it took focus to figure out ways to pass the tests.

When it was homework time, I simply didn't do it. Ok, maybe a little here and there. Math was alright. If it had anything to do with reading or spelling, I just wasn't capable, not much different than a kid who is not athletic.

———

When I was in early high school, I came home so drunk once that I puked in my bed. That was the first time my mother made me clean it up! I was very grateful she never gave me a lecture, just a lesson about getting too drunk. Why? Because they drank cocktail's every night and beer after.

I started smoking pot when I was 19. My mother couldn't understand why. She said, "We have always let you drink, and dad even purchased *Boone's Farm* wine for you."

The other part of this story is one of my parents' good friends' son smoked pot in Vietnam and then became a heroin junkie. Of course, they blamed marijuana, and there was no mention of the trauma of the war experience. This also ignored the fact that a close neighbor's son was killed in the heat of the war while my brother Dennis was serving his tour in Vietnam. Mom never said another word after that.

Sometime during my high school years 1966-1970 our home heating converted from a coal fire hot air heater in the basement to hot water baseboard. I soon realized I could convert the old coal bin storage space into my new bedroom. My good buddy and I hiked through the woods to the clearing where trees that we played in as kids were being cut down for new single-family homes. We grabbed a few 2x4's and some sheetrock. I think these were the last things I stole with the innocence of a kid.

It was easy to imagine that I needed wood pallets to raise the floor off the slab because the basement sometimes flooded in the rainy season. I acquired some used carpet, a mattress, small electric heater, black light, some blacklight posters, albums, and good speakers.

My parents were now two floors up and usually in bed by 8-9 pm. There was an outdoor cellar door access to the basement, so no one had to go through the house or talk to my parents. For a few years we smoked a lot of pot and listened to albums, surrounded by posters and a black light. Mom or Dad never once called my name or came down in the evening.

Feelings

Let it rip! What is there to lose? Here, sensitivity is the key. We are all different. It's taken me 42 years and hundreds of lifetimes (likely more) to get to this point. Why should I think everyone else should already be here? I don't, it's just my point of view.

It's my story from head to heart. As I feel sharp and intense pain in my neck, down in my shoulders, deep on the right side, in the blindness of pain, I sense my mother. She is looking at me. I look back for the first time, deep into her eyes, and hear her say,

> "I hurt, I am falling, and no one understands the pain of my life. Though in the outer world all looks well, I live in hell. Who could reach out and touch me if it wasn't my husband? I love him dearly and he loves me, but to touch the place of my pain, I know of no one. To be left alone is my greatest fear."

Mother, I had only an inclination, and I was out on the edge myself. So, I can love you now, and I can see your eyes are clearer as we try to connect. The pain is real as we feel and then release it. Poof, it's gone. In that way the experience is worth every penny. We can let the pain go. It's OK with me. Did you get out of this lifetime what you intended or hoped to learn? I think you did. I bet you were surprised to see your friends waiting on the other side.

The Other Side
Dawning of the Age of Aquarius

We remain where we are until we realize our state or condition and decide to change. Perhaps the Buddha said, "The source of all pain is attachment" because we know we can't take it with us. Our earthly power over objects and other humans on the mental and emotional levels doesn't hold water on the other side.

On the "other side" simply means we are no longer occupying a physical vehicle in the third dimension. It's like a scuba diver enjoying life underwater until the air supply runs out. Poof, we are still the same person minus the underwater vehicle. The inner thinking and feeling part of our self remains the same minus the physical body.

In the animal world many creatures require eating smaller creatures to keep their bodies alive. That is animal nature for some and perhaps the reason for all the wars and killing throughout history. There was little thought given to the afterlife. Most humans were very simple minded and easily manipulated by the king's army.

Once on the other side, we are still who we are, our thinking and feeling consciousness is still the same. If we were kind and loving, trusting and helpful in our time on earth, we find ourselves among others who think, feel, and act as we do. It is the same for the so-called evil doers. Imagine all the selfish, greedy, abusive personalities stuck in the same room, trying to exist with each other in the eternal light. They are mired in the muck of their own making. Because what appears in this physical world eventually disappears, the power we had over others becomes nil. What a shock to the system!

The universal law, "we reap what we sow" means we are eventually rewarded or "punished" and taught a lesson because of how we treated others. Therefore, to love everyone makes the most sense from the larger view of reality and means we remain in a state of love instead of hate. It doesn't mean we don't do what is necessary in a difficult situation.

To become free and change direction we need to realize what needs to change and start cleaning up our act. This is an example of reaping what we have sown. Make hell for others in this life and you will experience hell on the other side and be sent back into incarnation to learn about cause and effect. We will experience what we have done to others.

It can be a major shake-up in consciousness to find

oneself in a place we never anticipated, so it's an advantage to seek within while living in the world. Life on the other side is "eternal," and our new energy body consciousness no longer has the need or ability to fall asleep. Its 24-7, there are no clocks, no sleeping, and no day and night. It's all light, all now, present moment. This can be daunting to ponder and experience. This is a reason to find time to develop a healthy practice/art that grabs our attention.

The thought arises, "Well, we need stuff/money to live." True, we need food, healthcare, and shelter, which are basic needs for the physical body to survive. Once that healthy foundation is established humanity will start healing.

We will end the horrors of third world conditions, a condition that humanity must learn how to heal. As all human life starts to improve, the need and cause for a third world population will come to an end. There will no longer be a need for "new souls." New souls are created when a child is born and no other existing human, who are out of incarnation, needs that life experience. If we no longer have "newborn souls" the lower grade levels will eventually no longer be necessary. Humanity will lift its consciousness. Wars and poverty will eventually come to an end. Truly there will come a time when humanity is happy and healthy across the globe. When? Maybe it will take hundreds of years to get the balance.

We have no exact idea how much longer this "us against them" attitude will last. The gods can't come down and fix it for us. They do send us teachers, but it is something humanity must work out for ourselves. More people need to rise to power in "service to humanity" instead of "service to money and power. It is the dawning of the age of Aquarius.

Masks

People can hide their intent behind a mask. It appears we are moving too fast as a culture. Culture would have us believe that our happiness is directly related to the economy of our home nation and world. When the culture keeps people suppressed in the material world, finding our soul becomes the challenge and purpose of our life. The soul is our essence, the part of the self that waits in full awareness for the opportunity to operate through the physical form of the body and personality walking on Earth.

When things are out of balance they are revealed and often hidden at all costs. The path is narrow when we walk internally and face what we can no longer avoid. Unconditional love is the ultimate attitude and perspective.

Gratitude is strong medicine to carry. It feels better

when we resonate with gratitude. Resentment never pays well in the long run or even in the short run. The sooner we can get over feelings of resentment, the better it is for all those affected. If we learn our lesson, the next time the situation presents itself we will step through the experience holding mental and emotional clarity. How we resolve inner battles determines the playing field for the next time we are presented with a similar situation. I may wish goodness for everyone, but I am also conscious that not everyone embraces my ideals. I may love everyone, but I do not trust everyone.

The gurus of the past would send the disciple into "The Cave" for long periods of time to explore the inner worlds, affording the disciple the luxury of no outside distractions. In 1975 I was told these days of the solitude were over and it was time to do the work in the world of human relations. Finding the line between trust and stupidity can be a difficult lesson. The disciple needs to balance love and understanding. Taking time to do inner work is like tending a garden, it's a commitment.

We always feel our vibration according to the quality of our soul filtering into the human form. To know a peaceful mind means we now perceive the world in a conscious way. We are aware that we are aware, and only we have the ability to take charge of our life.

A spiritual practice is developing the strength and consciousness to remain present. It's not like we come to earth and are subject to a culture that is highly creative, balanced, and healthy. We are born in a world at its wits end, where the mass education of the populace is focused on material gain, earthly desire, the need for money or the right or left political views.

The River

These changing times in the flowing river of life require adjusting our daily work. We can begin with one conscious breath and a wish to do whatever is necessary. Much depends on where we are at the moment. Everyone is in a different place, yet many of us are in similar situations. The present condition of our body, mind, and emotions speaks directly to the tools needed to find and keep our center. Learning to find and keep our center is our daily work, but without good tools we are likely to find ourselves up shit's creek.

When we talk about finding our center, we are talking about finding the place within that can remain calm and clear in the middle of still waters or raging rapids. How we learn and develop that ability depends on the amount of energy and the quality of the teaching and guidance we have found.

Although it appears that many are out of balance,

we need to realize that this may be the best possible situation to wake up humanity. Important as it is to focus on a career and supporting ourselves, it is equally important to focus on personal inner development. Losing our joy for the sake of making a living is damaging to our ability to let our soul manifest through our personality and physical form. It may be helpful to find a teacher who can offer help along the way. It is also important to realize that at some point you must graduate and actually find the center on your own--finding our center should be the number one focus in life.

One day I was sitting on the beach, looking out over the ocean when something very strange happened. The ocean seemed to become a wide river. I searched the eyes and faces of those around me, asking the question," Do you see the river?" I felt on the verge of insanity; my mind was racing at 1000 mph. One day I was up the next day I was down; I didn't like it. And yet, I recognized that it had been my choice to jump in the river.

I can laugh now, 40 years later, but at the moment I was very serious. Not only could I see the river, but I also stepped into the water and felt the gentle current. I remember splashing in the water in an attempt to get the attention of others, so they would be aware of the existence of this river. They paid little attention, so I eventually turned toward the wide river and walked towards the middle. It didn't take long before the current carried me downstream and away from the world I had lived in before.

This was a major shift that required surrendering into the unknown. All I knew about the river was that it existed, and up until that point in my life no one had told me of its existence. I wonder why this was happening around the time I started to read *Jonathan Livingston Seagull* by Richard Bach.

Floating Downstream

April 19, 2011

Our thoughts are not who we are, but we find ourselves where our thoughts left us off. The one you deal with when you are alone in your bed is who you are now. Within and without are one in the same when we live in balance. We discover the world within when we let go of the things we are not. We can clear the path ourselves, or the universe will force us to face it sooner or later.

We can choose to live in the world of the consuming culture and seek the world within ourselves at the same time. It shouldn't be overly stressful to live and work. We create our own reality. The key is what we should seek first—the answer is not in the economy.

I no longer needed a priest to clear my way to heaven through the Catholic confessional. Confessing my sins to a priest so I could clear my soul of sin became a joke. The river is life on the inner side of our consciousness where inner conversations eventually play out in the external world. I am grateful I had that awareness and took that step when I was young and foolish.

The commitment to let the river carry me downstream was like becoming a child in a new world where the rules are directly connected to universe. In other words, I was totally consumed in a different reality. During my years floating down the river all things were given so long as I did my inner work. At first it was wonderful but soon the current started to speed up. I could see and feel I was heading into the gorge, so I swam to the middle.

I think I was aware of the quote in the Bible by Christ, "Unless you change and become like little children, you will never enter the kingdom of heaven," (Matthew 18:3) And where Jesus says, "For the kingdom of God is not something that can be observed, but it is within you." (Luke 17:21).

To the best of my knowledge Jesus never said to look anywhere else but within ourselves. That is also why we are told to "Store our treasures in Heaven and not on earth." (Matthew 6:19-21). The Buddha said the source of all pain is attachment. In other words, we can't take anything with us but the love and wisdom we have gained in this life.

My being is eternal. Age has little to do with the experience. And it's happening all the time from the perspective of the soul. Imagine if the world's wealthiest people decided to serve humanity instead of themselves. This is how we bring the Kingdom of God "On Earth as it is in Heaven." This concept, found in the Lord's Prayer (Matthew 6:10).

We must remember that our soul is eternal. Physical, mental, and emotional lives can repeat for millions of years. Our work is to wake up to that reality and begin the process of spiritual growth that consists of internal realizations and awakenings.

Eventually we will have leaders who will serve humanity's interests. People are different but the differences don't need to cause problems, let alone war. We will gain a deeper understanding and serve the greater good for all. What feels better than love? Some people love power over others for selfish reasons. The us against them mode of behavior needs to be replaced with a way to work together as a country and world before we can establish the Kingdom of Heaven on Earth.

Present physical world conditions focus on a body that will turn to dust. Of course we pay money for books, lectures, workshops, and bodywork to help us in our search. It requires that we give it attention internally. We are going within ourselves, alone.

Conversation

February 12, 2012

I can respond to the question of why the aliens have not come openly to us in the last 100 years. We were in the process of working off our karma. What that really means is our karmic load was so heavy that the Christ, not Jesus, pulled some strings and spread our karma out over the last 2000 years. He did this because the weight of our karma was so heavy that we could no longer move. That time is over, we worked off our karma and the hard nasty lessons are no longer needed. We are ready to move on in consciousness and general understanding of our situation as humans.

I feel we could use the aliens help to make this shift in consciousness. Something like a major LSD trip from the 60s and 70s. The mass consciousness is so dense that we need a blow to crack the egg. Maybe the egg is already cracked, and we just need a little help breaking it out! Either way it makes sense for the aliens to show up at this time. What a ride this will be, religion will fall away as we see, feel, and understand the reality of energy and the meaning of living in the present.

It's possible some outside intervention may be needed to help make the shift happen. What if we did have a reappearance of a Christlike figure? What if that figure appeared out of thin air and started to talk with you? For the time being, the power of the oil, food, and war machine will continue. It's a big subject.

These are beliefs and actions of a man with a mind on fire and a heart that knows nothing of the ways of love. There are many in places of power who have sold their soul for power in this physical world. They will do and say anything because the heart was turned to ice in the exchange. They cannot feel or see that humanity is one spirit. Forgive them for they do not know what they say. They are puppets of the dark forces. Forgiving simply keeps our hearts open and loving, but it doesn't mean we shouldn't aim for justice and elect someone better.

Reincarnation

The teachings of reincarnation have been with humanity a long time. According to an article on Wikipedia, "The first textual references to the idea of reincarnation appears in the *Upanishads* of the late Vedic period, (c. 1100 – c. 500 BCE), predating the Buddha." If it becomes common knowledge that reincarnation is a reality, and we become consciously aware that we "reap what we sow," the general consciousness and basic human understanding will be that each lifetime is one day in God's school.

It's not about accepting Jesus, and poof, all our troubles disappear. The Christ said, "Your sins are forgiven." True. What does that mean? It certainly could mean that God is not holding your sins of the past against you. It means we are welcome to start walking forward in our search for the "kingdom within," and we will be given the necessary lessons according to our karmic situation.

It's as if we lived inside a walled community, and one day the gates opened, and we were free to explore. Yes, we need to make a living in the world. We must do something to survive, but what we are doing? And what are we doing at the same time to explore our inner reality?

In February 2022, the Vatican released statistics cited on Wikipedia, showing that in 2020 the number of Catholics in the world increased by 16 million to 1.36 billion. That means that 17.7% of the world's population is Catholic.

———

I think I was 22 when I was introduced to the concept of reincarnation. This really blew my mind as I started to see that reincarnation and karma are intertwined. It explained how we can seek first heaven and be given what we need along the way. This explained how the "reaping" part of our sowed "actions" in one life could be carried over to the next. Clearly this spelled out a reason why we should act in ways to bring goodness to all. The quality of thought and action is followed by the energy of that vibration. It's not God's blessing; it is the law.

I started to see that our reality changes according to the attitude we hold, and that Jesus was correct when he said we would not get into heaven unless we become as little children. It is hard for some adults to believe the river we played in as kids still exists. The river doesn't age and will take us to places within ourselves that the normal culture avoids.

Our life continues regardless. Our control on the river is like a surfer, adjusting our attitude and approach to meet the needs of the present situation, or the size of the wave. I may wish goodness for everyone, but I am also conscious that not everyone embraces my ideals. I may love everyone, but I do not trust everyone; especially when it comes to the vulnerability of my inner child. The child still needs to play and be protected even if we are adults. Playtime diminishes as we age but its value becomes precious.

Play time allows us to enjoy the pleasures of being naturally high because it short circuits the internal chatter and allows us to be carried by the current of the moment. This is where our inner child lives. We visit him or her when we play alone or with friends.

The adult is charged with the care of the child within without external supervision. Our life will continue regardless. Good actions protect the children. The adult must provide the time and the space for the inner kids to play. Play allows adults to lighten up and realize that if they are spending too much time focusing on material gain an imbalance with the self is created. Lots of money can provide great distractions but, in the end, we will face our avoidance of self. The craziness is all manmade, including money. What would it take for everyone to have enough?

It is good to be able to juggle all the things in our life and it is also good to take a break. I think a healthy dose of play brings the river directly into the adult's life. Let's take a walk. Any control on the river is found in our ability to adjust our attitude and approach to meet the needs of the present situation.

Our Choice

At birth we wake in a body that vibrates within the visible light spectrum of our physical eyesight. What few can see is the aura that emanates from our body into the unseen frequencies surrounding our form. Like the hidden wireless Internet bringing information through the walls of our home, we are now aware that not seeing something doesn't mean it is not there. Mothers know things about their children the moment they walk through the door. Why? They perceive the world around them through the aura as a hand can feel the pleasure and pain of touch.

Today we are more than 23 years through the transitioning between the 1987 Harmonic Convergence and the Winter Solstice of 2012. We are leaving behind the mindset of out of sight out of mind for a world where we can no longer hide selfish deeds. The energy of our time is changing rapidly as knowledge becomes directly available. This is reflected on the World Wide Web and more so as we come to understand that our personal wireless receiver that connects us to the unseen world is through our aura. As the computer needs spyware and antivirus protection software, we need to protect our energy field from the crazy minds and violent events of our time. I first came to this realization when I was twenty.

The Passing

"If we only knew, we would welcome death and dread being born in a baby's body that knows nothing and can't care for itself."

The Tibetan Master Djwal Khul

As I write this, today is the five-year anniversary of my wife Deborah's death. The moment is more poignant as I learned this morning that a good friend who had been part of our lives before and during the four-year journey of her illness died today. This makes the feelings of loss and the sense of significance deeper.

Deborah's long battle with stage four cancer, and all the accompanying treatments, was a super intense experience. I'm flashing back to nine years ago with the diagnosis and how it all began. I remember that the first week or ten days friends invited me to dinner each night while Deb was in the hospital. Then treatments began with plans to review her progress with doctors for more treatments down the road.

The love of my life had learned she had stage-four cancer in the breast and brain. "Silence like a cancer grows," from *The Sound of Silence* by Simon & Garfunkel (1964) comes to mind. Facing the death of a loved one is one the most difficult experiences in life. It goes directly to our attitudes and belief structures regarding life and death, and challenges how we move through the process while someone very close to us is slowly fading.

In the beginning, a kind of numbness took hold. Maybe it was a calmness created by the fact that the life path we were on suddenly stopped, shifted out of the blue, and reversed course. The life river that had flowed in one direction suddenly and radically changed course.

Once she was home, we were totally consumed, and I was basically on call 24-7. I spent most afternoons writing or playing guitar in another room in the house. If everything was calm, several times a week around five o'clock I drove down the road for a draft beer and a slice of pizza or salad. In the evenings, we often watched old TV reruns like *Beverly Hillbillies*, *I Dream of Jeannie*, and *Gilligan's Island*. We sat close together on the bed until we started getting repeat shows--it was a healthy and pleasant distraction.

More than a year into the treatments Deborah started feeling somewhat normal. She could drive, visit friends, or go to the store. That lasted about another year, and during that time, about once or twice a month for three or four days, I would go on a little retreat with friends. We mostly played disc golf, camped at the lake, or just hung out by the fireplace in Pagosa Springs.

I discovered that talking about death freaked a lot of people out. They avoided the topic as it churned up uncomfortable thoughts and visions that were filled with emotions. We've heard stories, or experienced first-hand, the emotional condition, or mental state, of someone struggling with great loss. Compassion for our brother or sister comes to mind.

There was a lot of alone time, meaning our minds and bodies were not as connected as they once were. After a while, she started getting weak and slowly sinking. I remember the morning we were getting ready to drive to Santa Fe for a treatment when she fell in our mudroom, trying to put on her shoes. Somehow, we managed to get her into the car for the drive. Upon arrival they took her straight to the hospital where they took X-rays and discovered she had broken her hip. That was the beginning of the end. After several days in the hospital, she was transported back to Taos, but instead of coming home, they took her to the Living Center.

The Center was close to the hospital and nearby and across the from the Taos Midwife Center that I built as general contractor back in the mid-1990's. So, it was a familiar area of town. Having lived in Taos for almost forty years it was easy to recognize familiar faces. In many ways I felt at home. After a few weeks I became a regular and soon realized that most of these folks did not have many visitors. I learned that if I just greeted someone with a smile, and an acknowledgement of their existence, they remembered me the next time. It became a joy to visit the center.

Just a month or two after Deborah was admitted, another Deborah, a friend I had known for forty years in Taos, was admitted just down the hall. With that came a stream of visitors and very old friends going back to the Guru days of the 1980's. One of the main teachings of the Guru was to love everyone. He taught us to send healing light and love to everyone, and to be grateful for every experience. And so it was that I was given the opportunity to beam love to everyone I encountered. In some weird and unexpected way, going to the Living Center became like going into the temple to pray and meditate.

I visited Deb twice a day unless one of her soul sisters visited her. I sat close by in a chair. Early in the process we could talk, and she could use her cell phone and computer, but that only lasted a month. She lost all her beautiful long red hair because of the treatments that went directly to her brain.

Three and a half months after Deborah was admitted to the Living Center, we agreed that she was going to die and switched her status to hospice care for the last several months--same room, same bed, just a different set of procedures. Bless all the workers who came to work every day with a smile, or at least a good attitude, as they served humanity.

Four months later she was in and out of consciousness. What an educational experience. Her soul sisters and I took turns, sitting in the room and watching over her. I sat next to her and watched what went on around me.

There were only a few people in our life who visited Deborah while she was in hospice. I understand this. I remember one friend said, "I don't want to visit her because I want to remember her when she was healthy." They might not have felt close enough for such an intimate exchange. The friends who visited were our sisters on the soul level. In some important way, they came to my rescue. I had a little "time off" where I could visit a friend, play guitar, or go out for an evening meal.

It is interesting to me as I recall my friend, who passed on Deborah's 5-year anniversary, once told me that he didn't want to visit her in hospice because he wanted to hold his beautiful memory of her. In my imagination, I can now see Deborah greeting him on the other side, looking more beautiful than ever--this brings a smile of joy.

I feel blessed to have had the four-year experience with Deborah. We had time to process, and we had time to just be. Deb faced her death directly, and I was there to support her, doing my best to remain present, calm, clear, and loving. This felt like a call to arms. Everything esoteric or spiritual that I learned and practiced and had come to believe as "reality" over the last 40 plus years was put to the test.

Day by day our communications dwindled. The last communication we had was when I asked her, "Do you know what's happening?"

Deborah said, "I am dying."

———

The evening of March 12, 2019, I got the call a few moments after I had turned off the light for the night. I dressed again and went to her room at the Living Center to be by her side until they came and took her away.

There had been time to prepare for Deb's departure. During the last ten days I remember siting close by her side and talking to her about the inevitable. Of course she couldn't respond, mostly if not always her eyes were closed, and I imagined her slowly lifting off, slowly cutting the last of the cords connecting her to the body. She was remarkable, she was fearless, and it was clear that I should be grateful for her release.

Some days later I retrieved Deborah's ashes. She was free and had returned home, but what to do with the ashes? And then I knew, because early in our relationship I had taken her boat camping at a remote lake in New Mexico. I recall she said it was like the Garden of Eden. I returned to the spot and climbed to the highest remote place overlooking the lake and let her ashes soar.

A few weeks later we had a *Celebrate Deborah* party and all our friends gathered--what a wonderful experience. The atmosphere was filled with a vibration of love as people shared stories and experiences they'd had with Deborah. I was overwhelmed with gratitude.

Over the years since her death, I've been asked how I was able to maintain a relatively calm and positive state while Deborah was slowly passing. Many said told me they could never do what I did. Why? I believe it has something to do with a conscious perspective on death. If we think and believe, "I could never do that," or "we could never know," and continue to hold onto that belief, that is where we are. We have concluded that we could never know, thus the inward seeking of understanding stops, and our attention goes to another place.

At first, I felt sucker punched by the experience. "This was not in the plan!" Or was it? And if it was in the plan, what is or was the purpose? The gift? The teaching? What was the lesson to be learned?

The Gift

Deborah was the gift, especially in the way she handled herself. A caregiver could ask no more, and perhaps the caregiver was being gifted by Deborah. We shared a precious time together where we were much more focused. We tried to stay present and be grateful for what we had.

The Teaching

Several teachings flash through my mind. We realize that everyone who is born in a physical body will lose it eventually. The teaching is, *we are not our physical body*. Our body is simply a vessel to experience this third-dimensional reality. It's like a semester in college and then poof—we are back in our astral body and wide awake on the astral plane where it's light. There is no sunlight, all forms are of their own light, there is no shadow. Time, as we experienced it on Earth, no longer exists. We no longer need to eat or sleep--it's the eternal now. I understand that we are then in our etheric body, but most will understand the astral better.

We are greeted by close friends and teachers not presently in incarnation. These are soul brothers and sisters with whom we have experienced other lifetimes. It is a welcome home party. Imagine the friends and close relationships we've had over the last hundreds of lifetimes. We've all experienced countless possibilities, and it's a joyful reunion.

The Lesson

I had to accept that this is my situation and there is no getting around the reality. There is no room for denial, so make the best of it. It was an awakening to walk the halls of the Living Center. Over time I met most if not all the staff and some of patients. My job and spiritual practice was to bring a smile and a beam of love and light. That's what my Guru taught and that was the foundation of the practice over the years-- gratitude for every experience. This was the exam, so to speak.

How can you feel gratitude when your love is dying before your eyes? Well, that was the teaching from the Guru when I was in my 20's and 30's. The mantra, along with the teaching was, "I am grateful for every experience."

Growing up I don't remember hearing anyone talking about gratitude. Especially "for every experience." We probably heard, "I hope you learned your lesson!" True enough, but was there a teaching along with those words? There was no teaching or in-depth conversation, just a simple sentence spoken clearly, and usually with some emotion, as Mom or Dad said," I hope you learned your lesson."

After Deborah's passing, I was free in the sense that I was now alone with myself. I no longer shared a deep and intertwined soul relationship. Deborah was free of her earthly body after masterfully facing death, consciously, and with grace. I was, and still am, filled with gratitude for the experience, which gave me the gift of witnessing something so powerful that I can now share with others.

I remember George Harrison singing, "Give me light, give me life, keep me free from birth." (*Give Me Love* 1973). Thank you, George, for planting the seed of reincarnation way back in 1973. I know in my heart that Deborah and I will meet again in other lifetimes to continue our journey to the light.

Part Three

Yesterday I was clever, so I wanted to change the world. Today I am wise, so I am changing myself.

Jalal al-Din Rumi

Sunday Papers

This section can be read straight through, or just scan and choose a topic that appeals to you.

When I met the Guru Herman Rednick in 1975, he introduced me to the Christ Path of Love and Service. There was no charge for the teachings, but there were a few rules to be followed if one wanted to become a disciple.

The foundation of the discipline was no drugs, no meat, no alcohol, and the writing and reading of our Sunday papers out loud in class. We would gather early for chanting and rhythmic breath as we entered meditation. After some period, one by one we would individually read our written paper that was related to the lesson that was given the previous Sunday. Once that was finished, Herman would read a new lesson for the following week and we would write the topic in our notebooks.

There was a period for questions that was followed by a few beautiful songs by a disciple who had a beautiful voice and vibration. When class was over we were sent back into the world of daily life to practice our yoga. The essence of our practice was to do our best to maintain the calm mind and loving heart while being married with kids and full-time work in the world.

1. Spirit of the Presence
4/30/80

I am focused on love, Christ, and spiritual presence, and then I am not. I feel intensity and then it goes away. But still water runs deep and so it is with Spirit's presence in my life. Maybe I feel I am not moving at a fast enough dash, but that is a block if I dwell on it. Instead, I intensify my focus at this moment and every other moment that I remember. I should not feel guilty that I lost the moment to a wave of *Maya*. Instead, I rejoice when I find it again. I ask and pray with love and gratitude that the moment I spend in the spirit of presence we'll be close together next time.

2. Clear Channel
7/18/80

My life purpose is to be a Clear Channel for the Christ. To be transformed into this channel I must be focused with love and intensity upon the Christ. Within my family I find great opportunity to be of love and service, discovering my blocks and becoming aware of the love needed to dissolve them. Thus, I come upon a goal and something I wish to accomplish in the near future, to be a calm and loving channel for my child and beloved to be understanding and aware of their needs. Then with a heart on fire I will move into the world and help prepare for the reappearance of the Christ.

3. Design and Structure
7/27/80

I am grateful for the design and structure in my life. For within it I find the patience to walk the path of the Christ. I am like the seed of the flower. The flower will begin its journey to fulfillment when it is planted in a rich soil and forever on keep it roots firmly planted there. From the soil it will be given the nourishment needed to reach its destiny. From the state of full blossom, it is like the Christ giving never asking for anything. What the soil is to the flower the heart center is to my soul. So long as I live in its nourishment, I will grow like the flower first breaking through darkness into the light then forever reaching towards the Sun and sharing with no thought of self. I pray to be like the flower, unwavering in my focus to serve and be one with the Christ.

4. God's Will
8/3/80

I serve as I walk the path, helping a brother and walking the Christ path cannot be separated. Just as we cannot separate the process of our egos as we walk towards the city of God there is a rhythm and harmony around us at every moment. We begin to blend with it as we step on the path. We say, "Not my will, but thy will Lord." I see the will of God as rhythm and harmony and through love we give ourselves to this song. We are guided and we receive what we need, and we are led to those who are in need. In talking with a friend, she said, "It would be nice to have a social service job, then in my job I could be of service." I agreed but it does not matter what I do for a living if I live in the rhythm and harmony of God's plan, I will be serving. I will be guided, and I will become a clear channel for the Christ fire.

5. Plan for the Brotherhood
8/9/80

Where else would I find brotherhood but within my heart? I may acknowledge its presence but if I do not live it or feel it within, I will be separate. I focus on Christ when I remember I touched my brother with love. When I remember and as I remember a little more each year my life becomes less and less filled with thought and more and more filled with light and love. My thinking mind is finding brotherhood in my heart, and my heart is discovering the unity of brotherhood in everyone I meet. I am grateful for everyone, and the guidance of those in the unseen world that guides us every hour.

6. The Straight Path
8/16/80

Walking the path of service is a commitment not only to love and serve humanity but to love and serve Nature that surrounds us. The straight path is a path of balance moving in rhythm with the spiritual plan and in harmony with nature. In this day and age, we do not need to have the intense emotion of saint Francis shown embracing a leper, but we can take to heart his intense love and devotion for humanity and nature. We do not need to break away from society as he did. Instead, we work in the world as a clear and loving soul who knows the plan in his heart and mind. I see a brother being injured by a negative thought form every day, I will love him this week. I will speak truth when it is needed to be spoken this week, I pray to find the courage to live like Christ.

7. Open the Psychic Door
8/24/80

To be loving and clear away all resentment is key to becoming a channel for the soul that is focused on Christ. This pushes open the door to love in every situation, and this feels good and seems natural. I cannot justify in my mind or heart not to love. Strong thoughts of resentment and criticism may enter but not without consciously detecting their negative vibration. When these thoughts enter, I do not feed them with my focus, instead I try to send love and change my focus to a positive image, thus depriving the resentment of a strong foothold. I cannot say I am clear of resentment for as I become purified the resentment that was obvious clears away only to reveal more subtle forms. I see as I reach one mountain peak that there is a long chain of mountain peaks separated by trials and tribulations. Each are very different and yet very much the same, and there is a voice inside that says, "Be on your way son, you are to walk the path of the Christ."

8. Group Unity
9/12/80

I believe everyone is my brother, and in my heart and mind I know this is true, but within me there are different degrees of brotherhood. With some there is a clear and untarnished flow of love that is known and felt with one look in the eyes. But with others the flow is clouded by judgments and criticisms. I struggle to pour out love and to be at ease for I am acutely aware of the distance I have created with the negative thought forms. I remember telling my guru that getting up at 4:00 AM was the hardest thing I've ever tried to do. He replied, "That is nothing compared to stopping thoughts in the mind," In other words, that is nothing compared to waking up to the spiritual reality within and remaining awake to live and serve the brotherhood of man.

9. Our Meditation Group
9/21/80

I am here to serve, not to spend my time focusing on psychic phenomena. I am here to love, not to try to develop energy centers before their time. Herman told me if I open my heart in service and love the other centers will open naturally. I am grateful for this guidance. I used to think I wanted psychic experiences to let me know I was growing spiritually. Now, through the guidance of the Christ path, I can see my growth through my reactions to experiences. When I go through a difficult experience and remain loving and have understanding and compassion for those around me, I have made a step toward the city of God. As I experience and express love the spiritual world will unfold like the world unfolds before a child.

10. Is There an Easy Path?
9/27/80

I struggled with rising at 4:00 AM until I found an excuse to rise at 5:00. I worked on my list for a while and then it faded into the bookshelf where it has remained. This week I realized that I am not ready to be as intense as Saint Francis. I have other things to do. Maybe in a month I can begin to rise at 4:00 AM and work on my list but now the dawn brings a new light. To wait is to waste time if my focus on Christ is as strong as my focus is now on building my house, I would surely have a flame close to the intensity of Saint Francis. What can I do when I see and know what should be done and yet sit idle as another day passes? To love is my song, and if I were to rise at 4:00 am I would have time to work on my list. That hour is a gift. It is mine if I will it.

11. Who is My Brother?
10/5/80

Walking down the street I opened my heart and the separation that existed turns to a vibration of unity and I see that we are one. I look in your eyes and I see myself. You speak to me, and if I am still loving and aware, it is a message from God. We play like brothers and sisters, and then my brothers and sisters become the divine father and mother as I learn from your actions. I shall not judge you for we are all part of one body. I shall not criticize you for your presence in my life it is a gift from God.

12. A Positive State of Mind
10/19/80

What is a problem but a dark cloud blocking our vision from our inner light? It's not a problem, It's nothing more than a situation and if we refuse to place a good or bad label on that present state, we will find that each situation brings up an opportunity to learn and not get confused when darkness hovers over our heads. These difficult situations should be welcomed for it gives us the opportunity to find and use the guiding light within. I am grateful for all situations thus I find in my life the rhythm and song leading me to the golden city.

13. Soul in the Instinctive Nature
10-25-80

I stand back and look with love in my heart and mind. I see and feel a new quality of consciousness. It is a small vision of unity, light, and love. Then within a minute I slip back into my separateness because I do not have the intense focus and love to sustain this state. And yet, I move in rhythm with the plan, and I see new experiences confronting and unfolding before me. At one point this week I tried to get mad at a brother for an inconsiderate act. As I did this, I observed the struggle between the soul and the "animal." The animal wanted to be mad, but the soul with a much clearer stronger voice would say, "All is part of the plan.

Be grateful." I know the soul to be true, yet I still roared for a moment when the opportunity appeared. I suppose the animal nature will play out its role until the soul fire pours unobstructed through this form. Lord, may I find the intensity needed to clear the channel.

14. The Straight Path
11/2/ 1980

My intensifying love for my beloved, and she for me, creates a union from which we can move out of our home and touch those we meet with love, wisdom, and guidance that comes forth from the spirit. Within this union is the key to the spiritual life. How fast we move towards the mountain is not my focus. I know the mountain comes to me as I love. I know Spirit fills my heart and mind as I serve without thinking about the rewards. The basic foundation for spiritual life is built and I have the key to transform the selfish thoughts and reactions to only kindness love and compassion. I see always the Divine Mother in my beloved and to see the Christ in the person on the street. In striving to make these words a reality I walk the straight path.

15. A Radiant Body of Light
11/8/80

As I sat this week and talked with my beloved

about our goals, we found many branches all leading to one main focus--to serve the Christ. The many branches deal with our beloved relationship and how and what we can do to blend our beings into one light moving towards God. As we come together, we shall blend with humanity and the Christ. I live to be united with the Christ spirit, and this physical form is only a vehicle on Earth. May I be free from attachment when I cross over.

16. Love is the Essence of the Path
1/17/81

Every human personality has shortcomings, if we are engaged in observing the imperfections of others, we deprive ourselves of the opportunities of learning from them. Remember that every being carries within itself the spark of Buddhahood, but if we concentrate on other people's faults, we deprive ourselves of the light that shines in various degrees from our fellow beings. These few lines broke a hypnotic hold for I do engage in seeing faults in some people and surely, I've missed seeing God when the presence was there. I was told to love because by doing so my brother becomes my teacher and my sister becomes the light on my path. Most importantly, this form can become a channel to help others find the way.

17. Ancient Mysteries
2/8/81

The opportunities and challenges set before us on this physical plane can be transformed into spirit. The problem of how I will pay these bills is answered by not losing focus to the confusion of money and finance. Maintaining the focus on Christ and remembering the words, "Do not worry about tomorrow for tomorrow will have ills of its own. By seeking first, the Kingdom of God all else shall be given." Freedom surrounds us every moment if we would be clear enough to see it. There is freedom within us when we stay focused on the Christ path the mysteries unfold along the way.

18. The Mayan Approach to Spirit
3/7/81

What will it take to sacrifice my ego and enter the city of God? I need to get rid of blocks that prevent the light of my soul from shining forth. At times the thoughts that speak so loudly say you can't love your beloved because of what she is doing. Can I ignore any sense of fear that arises due to lack of commitment and faith in the plan? I will find courage to speak truth when I know truth needs to be spoken. The sacrifice required is giving without measure and without looking for reward or growth. It is the process of becoming the Christ.

19. Time to Meditate
5/1/81

I am not satisfied with my life. How can I be when my mind and emotions are not focused on the Christ all day? How I can be at peace when I do not love all I meet and think about? I seek to love and serve, and the challenge before me is to live in the world and be in a state of meditation with every step I take. I must bring this state into my daily life--this is all I wish to care about. Morning meditation sets the tone. The price I pay when I break that rhythm is no longer worth the cost.

When the outer world takes control of my life, the song I sing reflects the material world and I don't live in a state of meditation. When I live with the spiritual focus my song is light and love, and as I walk down the street I am meditating. As I go into the store my song fills the atmosphere, and my brother is touched by the spirit presence that lives within me. I do nothing but set the stage the spirit sings the song.

20. The Body is a Temple
5/3/81

Thought has spirit and that spirit can be transferred to another. A friend told me of a negative image he had of a person we both knew. Now I hold part of that image. It all comes to light as we learn to understand the power in words. Silence is golden. A single word or phrase can heal or destroy, strengthen or weaken. Often, I hear unconscious negativity and criticism directed at someone. When I am clear I can see its effect on those around me. When I am not so clear, I can get caught in the ego game of separateness and talk negatively about others. Even if I do not speak yet I listen, smile, and laugh, I am guilty. I pray for strength to keep my focus and to avoid all negative and destructive conversations. I intend to always speak consciously with love for my words have power.

21. We Are Not Alone
5/24/81

I wish to serve the Christ as I walk in the world of

men. But how do I serve? It is by living the Christ life and serving through example. The example is found in my daily attitude of cheerfulness and harmlessness to all things in love and understanding. These qualities create the light within. It is what we need to move through the storms without losing the light. These qualities bring us closer to who we are.

I find it easier to maintain this state outside of my home where there is less emotional attachment. Yet it is my home that prepares me for the world. At home where my interactions are as close as my breath I struggle, my light flickers and I realize through gratitude that my experiences with my family are directed exactly where my blocks are. I have no doubt that my prayers are answered daily for when I wish to be a clear channel my blocks are revealed.

22. The Spiritual Path
5/30/81

What prevents people from turning to the light when they are in need? It must be a fear created in the mind that is living in illusion. What can I do but have love and compassion for this soul. I try to reach out, but the illusion is thick, and it hurts because this person is my parent. I try not to lose my center to waves of emotions and sadness. Instead, I retreat into my heart and because of the understanding the spiritual path has given me I love, and I find the compassion to serve.

23. There Are Many Paths
6/14/81

The path is simple and straight. I follow it with sincerity and devotion. When I found the path there was no doubt or confusion whether it was right or wrong. There are no ranks among us and no classes that will put me above you. There is love, service, and compassion. I move in accordance with what I give and as I give a veil is lifted from my eyes and I see more clearly. The Maya is still thick, but I see a beam of light penetrating through the darkness. The light brings security through service and compassion, and my heart opens to my higher mind and soul as I walk this path.

24. Clear Vision
6/20/81

I say, "Lord I want a clear vision," and a voice responds, "Are you doing your work?" The clear vision of spiritual love is here for the taking if you but work for it. I slip in and out of focus, mostly out of which allows for the vision of Maya and resentment to live and see through my eyes. I do not want this in my eyes any more than I want sawdust or dirt. It hurts and the world becomes blurry. Is my soul seeing through my eyes when I see the purity of nature and its beauty? It must be at least in part for at that time my heart is full of love and my mind is still. I strive to see beauty in all things, and I strive to love. I was given a vision this week that revealed an old pattern of coldness toward my beloved and a reoccurring situation. I was given the sight. May I remember this gift and use it in love as it was given.

25. With the Help of the Christ
7/12/81

What is it that I really want? I want to be more focused in love and toward my beloved. We have the spiritual focus present, yet I let countless hours slip by unfocused. I know I am not alone in this feeling, but that brings no comfort. I have the vision of where I want to be. I feel that vision when I am in my teacher Herman's presence, and I lose it all too often when I'm at home or work. I can't say I am looking for the answer because the question was answered years ago, and I can't find an excuse or alibi in my daily routine because the spirit is everywhere. It is my focus that brings the day's vibration. If I listen to my heart and my higher mind instead of my body, I will rise at 4:00 AM and begin to make a reality of the spiritual dreams and hopes I hold so dear.

26. What is a Beloved?
7/19/81

I do not feel upset or confused about the new concept in the beloved relationship. I feel clearer and more willing to go deeper. In spirit all people are one.

In spirit beloveds are one. In our movement toward this light, we blend in rhythm, harmony, and purpose. My beloved's tone brings out feminine vibrations in my being and I for her. We find within each other those qualities that will bring forth the completeness of our being that blends the male and female aspect. I do not feel discouraged if we may not spend the next life together because it is this life in this moment that I move toward God.

27. The Beloved Yoga
7/25/81

You give to me and now I give to those I meet and think about. I heard the truth before as it moved through my consciousness, or did I react in the manner the truth has been directed? I've acted only out of necessity for my own personal comfort and didn't see the importance in the teaching. You give of yourself so completely and I take because I am hungry because that's the way it works. I will return your gifts a thousandfold to our brothers seeking the path. Now I wish to act out of love and the will for spiritual union and service. It all becomes clear when I see the choice is mine. I am here to follow the path of the beloved for one reason. I seek completeness and this will come if I follow the instructions and love with all my might.

28. Divine Energy
8/2/81

During the week I concentrated on how I mold energy with every thought. Someone might say something, and my mind reacts and makes a silent comment. I saw resentment and criticism that I didn't know existed. I began to understand what the concept that energy is a sacred trust means. I am a creator and a being of power of a certain degree. When I think, waves of energy move through me. I can help create positive and loving states around me or the opposite. How subtle these thoughts can be. I am responsible for them. A light begins to shine brighter before me, and I wonder why I let myself become lax from the disciplines and instructions I receive from Herman. One week of intensity seems to have done more than months of being lax. I stand in the midst of God's creation and there is divine energy everywhere. I begin to sing, and I become more focused. I feel the presence and it is closer than ever before.

29. Group unity
11-1-81

What does it mean to make a commitment to the group? For me it is the commitment to live and serve humanity since this is our group purpose. It is also working to love each individual within the group. Such love and unity is brotherhood and will become a living fire upon this planet. As I love you my brother and sister and you love me, we will be able to extend our boundaries. When Herman talked about dim lights and sparks among us, I wondered what I am. I felt that to be a spark would be the greatest goal. Then my life would be filled with day and night service. I feel the new tone about me, about us, as I bring my life into spiritual rhythm and focus. I am grateful that the desire to serve in the vision of the plan grows deeper each day.

30. The Eternal Word
11/15/81

The earth shall pass away but the "word" shall remain. To find the word, to live with the word, is a goal. To bring love into every situation is my purpose now. The word and mysteries will follow. There is no need to search for anything except the love in the heart for my brother and sister and to see the Christ in every face. I will store my treasures in a heart seeking only to love. To desire things of the earth and of this physical body keeps me bound to the material plane. After I crossover Christ gave me the key and I opened the door. I looked within and asked, "What matters to me? " My answer is to love and not fear the holy vibration that is transforming this personality into a radiant channel of light and love.

31. My purpose
11/22/81

During a difficult time in my beloved relationship

the vibration changes and intense love seems hard to find. But the love we have is deep and despite the difficulty we are connected as strong as ever. There is gratitude for the things that get stirred up as it is one more opportunity to transform our personalities. During the week I felt joy when I greeted a man behind a counter. He said he was glad someone was feeling good. Another man has lots of money but never have I seen happiness on his face. Next time I'll remember to send him love. And there was a drunk hobbling across the street, I thought, "When he crosses over, he will find himself in a bar reaching for a drink." I sent him love. Truly at every corner there is an opportunity to serve. How could I be anything but grateful for every experience? That Christ lives within my heart. Nothing of this world can steal it or tell her to leave. The Christ is life.

32. Your Future
12/1981

Seek first the Kingdom of God and all else shall be given. In these words, I base my life. There is no room for fear of the future and no room for worry about the things I will need. The great teacher of experience has proven to me that everything works out for the greatest good. To fear the future shows insecurity and a lack of sensitivity to the spiritual vibration that guides our lives with its silent voice. Unshakable faith with a strong focus and desire to grow closer to God is the first step on the path. From then on it becomes the food and clothing for every step hereafter.

33. Healing
12/20/81

As with most things, the spiritual path's answer lies in the heart. What is the quality of love that pours forth to my brother in need? Whether I heal a person or not isn't the point of sending healing. There are other forces at play. Look at Herman from my view, he had a long difficult recovery surely, he has the love needed to transform his physical trouble. I suppose this was part of his process as it was for Jesus. Cherokee Medicine Man Rolling Thunder said he takes three days to investigate a person before he heals them. Two things that would stop him from helping someone are the person's karma or attitude. I send healing at a low level compared to that of Christ healing the leper. It may not appear to be doing any good, but I am not the judge. The discipline of sending healing helps open the heart to love and in that way, I help heal the world.

34. Service is a Way of Life
12/27/81

As I walked the path, I discovered many are close to walking the path, in fact they already are. There are many who still do drugs and there cannot be a judgment because their hearts know and feel love and give it freely. They may not be as focused, or have the commitment we do, but their effect on the world is still positive. In my work I often have the opportunity to meet and work with people. I am learning to discover how strong they are attracted to the magnetic pull of the spirit. Nearly everyone believes. Some are truly seeking but can't quite let go of the world. The world still overwhelms others--what can I do? I love them and if it feels right, I talk of spiritual things and the path. It is our work to lead others to the path. A word today may help a friend, and ten years from now love may bring him the awareness to help others find the way.

35. A Focal Point
1/24/82

How do I increase my focus so I may become a devoted disciple who is worthy of becoming a focal point? The answer stands before me as clear as the Sun. To be a disciple the life must have total commitment to the path. Every aspect must be fused with love and spiritual focus. I can say a million times I am committed and devoted, but words are not enough--it is actions that speak. Herman gave us the tools and reminded us week after week. I remind myself every day, but if thought is not followed by action there is little movement. Work on the list twice a day and use introspective writing. Meditate twice a day and learn to see beyond the faults of others in love. My beloved, these are the things I must do. How devoted am I if I do not use these gifts.

36. Learning to Speak from the Heart
1/31/82

Take hold of this new intensity and direct it, that the will may be strengthened and our focus become more single-pointed. May our love dissolve the blocks and flow between us, so we may touch the world. Here is our gift, will we double it, triple it, or hide it away? When the Master returns, he will ask, "What have you done with the gifts I have entrusted you with?" The opportunity is great at hand and never will tomorrow be any easier if I do not love today. I say I want to love you, and I will. You my brother and sisters and my beloved are my gifts. You are great treasures, and I hold you in my heart.

37. The Design of Destiny
2/14/82

There are no accidents but there are positive and negative destinies that we create by our state of mind and heart. There is no blame for any negative state in which I might find in myself, I always have the choice to be positive and loving. It is the same in my beloved relationship. I cannot simply let it happen without an effort to communicate with honesty and clarity and recommit myself to love every day.

A great awareness came upon us this week when we realized we had a choice in our destiny. We chose to move forward together into more love. Any other path would only be a long detour, which in the end would bring us back to the place where we must love more to move forward. Together we will move into more love and light. We have the strength and guidance. My beloved you are blooming into a beautiful flower. I love you thank you for the many gifts of strength love and devotion. Gratitude fills me as I realize we are consciously awakening to the path we walk together.

38. The Image of God
2/19/82

I try to walk the straight path, but I take detours in the glitter and glamour that fills the sidewalks. It is hard to resist, and my attention gets scattered. If my faith was strong in the spark of God's flame, there would be no interest in the city lights. I have always thought faith was my strong point, but I realize today that if I was truly on the straight path the image of Christ would be there day and night. There would be no worry or concern about material life. I would love and serve and move in harmony with the plan.

39. The Great Commandment
2-7-82

The soul won't let the personality rise up without a struggle, so my personality comes up out of selfishness . I felt low, and it was hard to meditate. I said to myself, "What is important, holding onto ego or loving selflessly?" I'll admit I was clouded for a few days or was its weeks. "As you do to the least of my brethren you do to me."

Look what I do to my beloved! I saw what I thought was a fault that affected me, and I was not grateful for the experience. Somehow, I thought the experience she gave me was not what I needed for my growth. What an arrogant illusion! A spiritual view says you're the closest to me and it is through you I will find brotherhood.

40. Soul Fire

2/28/82

I was shaken out of an illusion to see the entire day spent without a concentrated focus on spiritual reality. Sure, I talked of spiritual things from time to time, but I was still asleep or at least in a fog. Oh, spirit soul within me I wish to know and feel your presence. I do not know if you are young or old, and that doesn't matter. I need to feel and know your presence. What will it take?

My soul replied, "Awaken and be conscious, put concerns of the world and body aside, all of these could pass tomorrow, I the soul will remain. Love your beloved, family, friends, and people everywhere. You are cared for; do you really think you have control? Arise at 4:00 AM and think of me, then through loving all day will reality open its door. Do not worry if it only attracts negativity. Be joyful and friendly to everyone. Send love and live in love. The answer is known, living it removes the thorn."

41. Lifespan
3/7/82

It seems like a dream because events and states of mind come and go. If it were not for the spiritual focus life would ramble on like an unclear uncontrolled dream state. Fill me with the existence of love and will and with the living example of the great power and light in Herman. How blessed we are to be in his presence. The only way to repay this gift is to prepare ourselves through love and will to one day serve as he does. He cares not of the suffering he bears but only that he can share the food he offers. I have so many personal cares that I hold in illusion. But Lord I am beginning to hear your silent voice when I listen with my heart, I am free I will never turn back I live to serve.

42. I Serve
3/14/82

The statement couldn't be more direct, if you don't do the work, it won't be done for you. You're not given anything you don't deserve. The days of taking the work halfheartedly are over. It was so clear to me while driving home from work. There is no rut or boring routine when I seek only to serve. I do breathe God with every breath and with it love and consciousness expand. I become more useful in the preparation for the return of the Christ. The work dawns on me as if I've been asleep for the past 29 years. The light reveals the work that must be done both on myself and in the world. Herman knows what he's talking about when he says work on your list and send healing. If you don't do the work, it won't be done for you.

43. The Fastest Way to the Temple Gate
3/21/82

Love is the vibration that keeps us alive. What an

opportunity we have here. What an opportunity that I must love you through all the mud. I know we both want to love each other. My awareness fades in and out, so brother, sister, and beloved I ask your help. If you see I am unconscious, please wake me up. Ask me what the mantra is this week or start talking about the work. Surely that will wipe the sleep from my eyes. I want to love you and see your radiant soul pouring upon your head and shoulders. Christ is my goal and these little selfish and criticizing thoughts are no longer welcome. Today I start anew, I know only that we want to love each other.

44. An Image
3/28/82

As strong as this lesson is it seems hard to find words, but I did learn much this week even if my focus didn't get stronger. In meditation I searched for the image that fits my being. The image carries the vibration that brings one closer to the energy pouring through the form of the Master. I thought, "How do I keep this image when I am concentrating on my work?" I don't. What I seem to do instead is carry the vibration in the tone of my being. I do my work with love but there are many times in the day and night when my mind drifts off, The image and the mantra are invaluable. Remember, being here in love we serve when we reach out and touch others with love . We grow spiritually when we serve with love.

45. Every Hour I live in God's Presence
4/11/82

Lord I am grateful for every person and event in my life. There is perfect rhythm and harmony. Love is everywhere. The requirement is that we let it flow through our hearts. Then it becomes obvious there are no accidents or coincidences. Nothing is out of place, and we receive what we need. Let there be no judgment in my heart toward a brother or my beloved. It is becoming clear that spiritual growth comes when we meet every person and situation with love and gratitude. Everything becomes a wondrous gift when it is greeted in the light of the soul.

46. The Path Through Illusion
4/22/82

Christ said it is not where you worship but how you worship. "And now is when the true worshipper shall worship the Father in spirit and in truth." (John 4:23). He also said, "A man is not defiled by what enters his mouth, but by what comes out of it." (Matthew 15:11). Herein lies the key to my path. I cannot judge another's vision of our spirit father. I do not have the love or insight to see clearly. If I could see clearly, I would not judge. How many times did I criticize the Catholic Church? Mother Teresa came from that path. I shall know my brother by his vibration and not by external appearances. We walk the Christ path of love and service, the path of acceptance of all people.

47. The Presence
5/2/82

I was clear, then as I lost faith as a cloud of confusion filled my mind. I had doubt and felt insecure. I knew these things weren't real, but I felt them. What do I need to do to keep my focus, so the clouds of Maya and negative voices do not fill my mind and bring doubt to my heart? Love surely is the key, but it must be blended with will. The will to love and the will to serve. The test for my will is to rise at 4:00 AM every day. Once a month is not enough. With will and love I can set up a rhythm when meditation is the same time every day. The meditation gets deeper, and I become more attuned with my soul. I can blend with all humanity. We share the same song. With will and love I can express harmony with every person I meet. This is the straight path we live in God.

48. Commitment
5/8/82

I seek to make my commitment to the Christ total. Where every cell of my being rings with the Christ and every action and thought silent or spoken has the Christ and the Plan in mind. How blessed I am to be able to sit in Herman's presence. His wisdom, vision, and love are unquestionable. I listen to what he says and strive to follow his instructions—they are my lifeline. It is difficult when my arms get tired and weak, but I ask what else is there to do? Personal gain is worthless, astral phenomena is worthless. It is the straight and narrow path, the razor's edge. So, I want to live in the vibration of the word, then I must be willing to obey the guru. I am willing beyond any doubt.

49. Freedom
5/16/82

Saint Francis did everything for Christ. That shows me where I am and how far I must go. I must investigate every situation and ask if I am doing this for Christ. If I can ask myself that question ten times a day, I'll be on my way to more awareness in Christ. The key begins at home. My Beloved and I open the channel for love and service when we are clear loving and making a deep commitment to the Christ path. This is the center from which all relationships stems. I seek to be warm friendly and a channel for Christ with everyone I meet. We are told what the world needs now is good human relations. It does not matter what I do or where I am, there is always a soul behind the personality to touch.

50. Your Commitment
5/30/82

There are no more valid excuses not to be focused, or not to rise at 4:00 AM. It seems like my life is entering the small end of a funnel. The wide circles are becoming smaller and faster, which leaves less time to wander off track. The only thing that seems of real importance are my family, doing yoga, and serving the group purpose. These three take in all my life. The goal is simple and straightforward--be loving and focused with every breath. It's hard work, some might say impossible, but what else is there? There is no time to waste. I've become more aware of my personality. I wonder if my ego is getting bigger because I feel I've made some movement. Or is it that the movement revealed more of who and what I am? I now choose not to be focused on personal gain but that I might be a point of light to help another find his way.

51. The Elixir
6/20/82

If it was up to my desire, I would wish that I could enter the city of God today. But I know that wish is only a dream or looking for some kind of free handout. It is said everything has its price. I hope to make it to the city of God in this lifetime. The price is to become focused like a point of fire, like the still flame of a candle. The wax of this candle is love, and the light of the flame is service to humanity. Herman you are the flame, the light, the love, and I think I understand you cannot turn me into the lighted candle. You can only guide me and show me how to do the work myself. You've said it a thousand times, "Disciples don't want to make the effort." I'm beginning to hear.

52. There is No Death
7-4-82

Will, focus, and love form the key to the world of beauty and light. Knowing this frees me from the dark clouds around the word death. We are told our focus must be so intense that if a stream of a thousand images passes before our vision, we do not get distracted. This is where I must work. The time to meditate it is not time to think of money, housework, or my job. So easily do these thoughts grab my attention. My Beloved, you bring light and beauty into my life. Herein lies another key, when I can see only the light, the beauty, and the divine in you every moment, then I will be focused enough to live in the higher worlds while still connected to this one. We can move into the world of light together.

53. Channel Between Soul and Body
7/11/82

How far will living these truths take me? I feel like I am only beginning, and yet, I'm already too far along to turn back. So here I am. I must transmute my nature and clear this personality of everything that hinders my walking the spiritual path. I must find my blocks and dissolve them with love and will. Block number one is lack of discipline! I need a will blended with love that is stronger than steel and as clear as Herman's eyes. How else could I stop the negative thoughts and emotions from entering and blocking the flow between the soul and this physical form?

54. Points of Reality
6/27/82

I must transmute the personality so that every breath of my life becomes the reality of light and love. It is not a thing to be turned on or off in difficult or different situations. Again, it is the point of fire and intense focus towards the divine that will bring me through the illusion into reality. Lord, I live when you live through me and in a world of a billion distractions, I need your help.

55. Many Fields
12/19/82

There are many paths to the golden city, but they are all paved with love. There are many rhythms, but they are all based on the will to love and serve. For a few months I had established an early morning meditation hour. Then I started to think, "Look Michael, you are finally doing it after all these years." I thought I would never fall out of it. Little was I aware that as I was saying these words to myself over the weeks I began to fall out of rhythm. In the beginning when I rose early with the will to love and serve the routine began to carry a new tone. When my personality started to pat itself on the back, I lost focus, and it became just a ritual. So, it is no surprise my meditation lost its intensity. There can be no thought of personal growth, I can only love my beloved family and friends with a calm mind and loving heart.

56. I Am a Disciple
1/9/83

The Path is my life and work. To walk this path is to accept the requirements of the master. He knows what will best prepare us to carry the light into the world. Our work is just beginning. There is nothing more important than the spiritual work and therefore no excuses can be made. I used to believe that I didn't have to work every day, I could get up at 4:00 AM. It was a lie and a lack of will. These disciplines carried forth with love and focus will attune our being to the master's vibration. I have noticed how at one time I could talk negatively about my brother and feel justified. Now, if I begin to talk negatively, I am sensitive enough to feel the vibration change, it is no longer justifiable. As I walked this path with more intensity, devotion, and love there is no doubt about my direction and there is no conflict of interest. This world holds nothing for me except the opportunity to serve the great Lords of fire.

57. Fulfilling the Plan
1/16/83

Now we have a group home and there is no doubt that it should be. We are being prepared to be world servers filled with selfless love and committed will. We will be open to the will of Christ. I am willing to put aside my individual goals to serve the greater group purpose. I fear not this change in our group. We are just moving from grade school to high school. It brings rushes of excitement for the next step is a large one. We have been prepared well. I am confident and know deeply that the master has done all he could. How great is our potential? It depends how selflessly we can give up our personal will to the will of the spirit. There is no limitation we can literally serve and affect the world from our center.

58. My Purpose
2/6/83

I am not this body. I realized this through consciousness of the loving heart and a calm mind. I walked this earth to serve humanity and transmute the lower nature I've lived in for many years. The sexual drive is the lower nature energy that can through love become divine. This is one we all struggle with. How can I transform sexual energy into divine energy with my beloved? My work is not to slip into pure physical aspect. I work to remember that this energy directed to anyone other than my beloved would be destructive to the beloved yoga and the path I walk. I seek to be in conscious control of this energy through love and will and not to have this powerful energy control my thoughts and emotions and therefore my body. This physical form is a temple for the Christ light; therefore, I will think no thoughts that will lock my consciousness into selfish material goals. We need not be limited by this form we need only to forget about it in selfless love and service.

59. I Am a Disciple
2/12/83

I can see the personality in my brother at times. This can irritate me, and a stream of criticism follows. When I see the personality in my brother, I can see his actions and his stream of love can flow from my being to his. Love quiets the mind and prevents the waves of criticism from coming into conscious form. I love you my brother and criticism does neither of us any good. Only by loving will this channel become clear. Criticism is no longer justified. I react to you in a negative way, and you are aware confront me if you wish. I seek only to love and to know you as a soul. Can I love everyone in this group ? Yes, I will it is the only mountain worth climbing.

60. The Plan
2/19/83

Master prepare me as you see fit. I will surrender my will to thine. The will and strength of Love is all I seek, and to find it is to use it in service. I will love my beloved beyond her personality, and from my home I will go into the world, remembering to see beyond all personalities. I will prepare for the return of the Christ by living and loving this hour. I will be harmless in speech and action and move in rhythm with the divine plan.

61. Living in the Moment
1983

There is no judgment or criticism as I grow when I love. How can I know what the next hour will bring? I live this moment as my mind wanders down streams of thought forms. There is no reality there, it is hard to stay in the moment, but only in the moment can I love. Only there will I survive the many dark clouds of Maya. We are here in the testing grounds and in God's school, only love will set us free. Brother, sister, I cannot resent you. There is no way, I know too much, I feel too much. It's been seven years. I've heard the simple and powerful words of our blessed Herman. I feel more love and gratitude than ever before. Love one another. Lord Christ, I pray for your reappearance by accepting every experience with love and gratitude. This is the way to prepare your presence.

62. The Master
3/5/83

The master is showing me the path to the temple. I hear some sound or voice, I do not need to travel far, where this note is within me. My awareness is focused on the present moment and how to be intensely focused on the spiritual path. He said it would be better spiritually to read the Tibetan's books than to see a spiritual movie. I hear and I understand that. I may still see a movie, but I got the point. I am ready to be that intense.

This narrow gate seems much smaller than it did last month. I think the words above the door before the temple gate says, "You can't take this world beyond this point." Am I ready for that? So, I'll sacrifice something in this world, anything in this world, if it would possibly help transform this personality. The point is to be a focal point of love and light, and the stimulation and inspiration must come from within. A movie will give you a charge, but the fire comes from within an intensely focused mind and heart.

63. A Temple
3/13/83

Words are hard to find for this lesson. I think of the blessings I've received from being drawn to this group, living within the eyesight of this holy temple, entering this atmosphere for early meditation, and absorbing the vibration that carries me through the day. What can I do to repay these priceless treasures? The answer is simple. I must learn to give as I have received from my master. There is nothing else in this world. I will love you my brother and sister until I see the glow of Christ in your heart. It is lack of love and focus that stands before me and this realization. We are disciples of the Christ and each of us has a plan to fulfill.

64. The Spirit Plan
3/20/83

All you have is ours to help us become clear channels. All I have is yours Master that you may use me in the plan you know and serve. The vibration you have anchored is the greatest gift. How will I use it? To hold it and try to hide it, I would surely lose it. I will go into the world and surrender my being that this vibration may touch others and double or triple. It is the greatest gift you have given and that we shall do greater things is the hope. As we become channels, we touch thousands and the gift you gave a hundred disciples will be multiplied a thousand times. It is this plan that the vibration will spread around the world as our work is for Christ. There is no room for self. The vibration spreads as we become clear.

65. Wesak Full Moon
5/8/83

What does it take to walk the path towards the city of God? Words are not enough. Good strong papers are not enough if the statements are not carried forth into the inner Wesak period. I have the will to love and to serve, but if I do not bring it forward into expression it is nothing. Lords of flame and your great sacrifice I cannot compare to thee, but I understand. I am about to go east for ten days, seemingly out of no choice of my own. But now I see I could go with or without the will to love and serve. The will to love and serve is my greatest potential. I need only focus on that, and a Clear Channel I shall become. Destiny provides the opportunity, but I choose what to do.

66. Earth Mother
4/3/83

Mother Earth, I have felt your presence in the mountains and when I lived by the sea you calmed my emotions, and my being began to feel the holy presence. I came from the noise and rumble of eastern life to live in the still quiet environment. But I am not here to escape from humanity, I am here to transmute this personality into a channel of love and light. One year or 25, I do not know how long it will take but if the time comes, I will be willing to move into the masses once more if that be the need of the spirit. But for now, I know the work that stands before me is to love my brother without judgment.

67. Clear Channel
4/10/83

Lords of Flame, great White Brotherhood, lead me on the path that I might gain experience to become a Clear Channel. To serve the plan is all I seek. For the past month my mind has been filled with starting a business, though these thoughts were necessary to make things happen on the physical plane, I realized I want to develop the will to control these thoughts. I do not want my consciousness to be filled with this material world. I seek only to love and serve my family, which starts with my Beloved and moves out to humanity. Blessed am I to be part of this group, this is my greatest opportunity, and I will not let it pass because of thoughts that try to make the physical life so important. Lords of Flame and Brotherhood I reach out to you that you might test me and that I might have the strength and love to become worthy of your divine influence.

68. Healing
4/17/83

I sit in class Sunday mornings and a wave of intense devotion washes over me. I want to do this work. I will rise at 4:00 AM and come to this temple and meditate. I will begin intensifying the love nature of my being and then move into the world. I believe now that I will find the master within. No other state holds an attraction except that of love and devotion. And I do not know what experience I need to prepare me to be of service. For at 31 I am still a child. I must have patience as I begin to intensify my love, will, and devotion. I cannot say what my spiritual work will be tomorrow, but today I know even if it is in the business of my daily worldly work, I extend a hand to a brother in the marketplace in a wave of love enfolds us. I seek only one goal and that is to become one with the holy being.

69. The Poem
April 1983

The pure desire to become one with thy holy being is what gives the disciple the attitude that all else is death and decay and glitter but for a moment. A fear almost comes upon me at the thought that I would want to live in this world and forget the spiritual. Lord you are my only reality. This world is but a dance I do to serve the Lord Christ, what else is there? I would surely go insane if I was to forget thee and worship the material pleasures. My sacrifice is not yet great. I hold on and think of myself for I still have a chain connecting me to the survival instinct. But I know Lord if I seek thee first all else shall be given. As a disciple I have different rules than the unconscious person. I need not think of myself for I know the loss of the personality is the caterpillar turning into the butterfly. I seek to live with one hope in my heart and that is to become one with the Holy Spirit.

One

Acknowledgments
The River Flow of life

Many thanks to my best friend and soul mate Roxanna Shores for all the love and joy we share during these years of transitions. I am grateful to artist Fred Collins, my bro and neighbor, for the art that led to the cover of the book.

Several years back I reached out to the universe for an editor who could esoterically understand what I had written and help clarify and aline the message. This wonderful soul is Julie Loar, author and editor. https://julieloar.com/

And thanks to my brothers and sisters over the last so many years: Bernie, Marybeth Norbert, Shari, Bob, Sue, David, Pam, Timmy, Fred, Linda, Armor, Patty, Juana, Mark, Caryn, Kit, Michael, Carolyn, Barbara, Kathy, Tim, Leslie, and other friends who we all know. I feel blessed and lucky to have shared life with you all on the many different depths we experienced together.

I am grateful to my daughters, Amanda, Michelle, Jessica, and your families for being who you are.

About the Author

Michael Carroll moved from New Jersey to Taos, New Mexico in 1975, to follow Herman Resnick, a guru with whom he studied for 10 years. He raised a family of 3 daughters and focused his life on creating strategies to help him navigate uncharted waters of growth and life choices. In 2017, Michael's book, *Into the Unknown, Life is Much More Than the Daily Grind,* Michael addressed the importance of pursuing a spiritual practice within each daily life. A practice that required us to look at how we live throughout each moment of our day. A practice which involved finding methods and concepts to ground ourselves as the rivers of change impacted the direction of our lives.

Michaels' new book, *Finding Balance,* represents a compilation of essays, transformative thoughts and undercurrents which directed and supported him to lead to a conscious life, thereby creating "a calm mind and a loving heart" in his daily practices.

A magical look into the world of how anyone can stay true to one's desire to create a life for a higher good.

Also by Michael Carroll

Into the Unknown: Life is So Much More Than the Daily Grind, 2017, Play More Better Press

Formatted with Vellum

*For my parents, brothers, partners, daughters, friends
and teachers along the way*

Copyright © 2026 by Michael Carroll and Play More Better Press

For more information or permissions contact

Play More Better Press * mcc@newmex.com

PO Box 4770, Tubac, Arizona 85646

Print book edition ISBN: 978-0-9991992-2-0

E-book edition ISBN: 978-0-9991992-3-7

Library of Congress Control Number: 2026901496

All rights and international rights reserved. No part of this product, including but not limited to any portion thereof may be reproduced, distributed, or transmitted in any form or by any means, including photocopying, recording, or other electronic or mechanical methods, nor may it be stored in a retrieval system, transmitted or otherwise copied for public or private use, without the prior written permission of the publisher, except "fair use" of brief quotations embodied in critical reviews and certain other noncommercial uses permitted by copyright law. For permission requests, write to the publisher, addressed "Attention: Permissions Coordinator," at the e-mail address above.

The intent of the author is only to offer general information to help you in your quest for greater personal and professional success. Buyers and readers agree that the publisher and/or the author are not engaged to render any type of medical, psychological, legal, or any other kind of professional advice. If you believe you need assistance, please consult a professional. Neither the publisher nor the individual author shall be liable for any physical, psychological, emotional, financial, or commercial damages, including, but not limited to special, incidental, consequential or other damages. You are responsible for your own choices, actions, and results.

Manufactured in the United States of America

10 9 8 7 6 5 4 3 2

Finding Balance

Navigating the Shifting Currents of Life's River

Michael Carroll

Play More Better Press

www.ingramcontent.com/pod-product-compliance
Lightning Source LLC
Chambersburg PA
CBHW050613100526
44584CB00037B/1873